D1561082

IMAGINING LOS ANGELES

PHOTOGRAPHS OF A 20TH CENTURY CITY

IMAGINING LOS ANGELES
PHOTOGRAPHS OF A 20TH CENTURY CITY

AMY DAWES, MICHAEL DIEHL, CARLA LAZZARESCHI AND STACEY R. STRICKLER · FOREWORD BY RAY BRADBURY

Stacey R Strickler

Amy Dawes '2000

Los Angeles Times
BOOKS

DEDICATED TO THE PEOPLE OF LOS ANGELES, PAST, PRESENT AND FUTURE, AND TO THE PHOTOGRAPHERS WHO CAPTURED THESE PEOPLE, PLACES AND MOMENTS IN TIME.

Editor: Carla Lazzareschi
Writer: Amy Dawes
Photo Editor: Stacey R. Strickler
Design: Michael Diehl
Research: Dan Lewis
Photo Scanning and Retouching: Imagic
Copy Editor: Patricia Connell

Los Angeles Times

Publisher: Kathryn M. Downing
Editor: Michael Parks
Book Development Manager: Carla Lazzareschi

Published by the *Los Angeles Times*
Times Mirror Square, Los Angeles, California 90053
© Copyright 2000 *Los Angeles Times*
All rights reserved. No part of this book may be reproduced without the written permission of the publisher.
First printing: June 2000
Printed in China
ISBN 1-883792-52-5

PHOTO OPPOSITE TITLE PAGE

WOMEN WITH AUTO CLUB DIRECTIONAL STREET SIGNS OUTSIDE THE CLUB'S HEADQUARTERS AT 2601 S. FIGUEROA STREET, LOS ANGELES

CIRCA 1945

Funneling new traffic into Los Angeles was the object of many of the thousands of signs placed throughout the state by the Automobile Club of Southern California from 1905 to 1956. Over the years, the Auto Club hoped, the signs would create the impression that "all roads lead to Los Angeles."

ABOVE

FAMILY AND FRIENDS CONGREGATE FOR FUN IN THE SUN AT SEAL BEACH

JULY 1921

Wide, sandy public beaches along Los Angeles County's 75 miles of coastline are part of the area's allure.

PHOTO ON PAGES 6-7

ECHO PARK LAKE LOOKING TOWARD DOWNTOWN AT DAYBREAK

1999

The projection screen for countless dreams and fantasies, Los Angeles can mirror those imaginings with a magic all its own.

CONTENTS

L.A. OUTTA THE WAY AND LET US HAPPEN!

RAY BRADBURY

GLANCING AT THE MULTITUDINOUS PICTURES in this book I see 10 million Angelenos marching to 10 million drummers, all different.

That's L.A.

New York? Ten million White Rabbits crying I'm late, I'm late, for a very important date.

Paris? A vast and beautific nose that too often scents fish.

But L.A. now. L.A.?

The true center of the world. Inventor of sport fashions for women with long lives and short skirts.

The absolute nexus of television. All TV is born or born dead here.

The absolute San Andreas fault line for films that crack the globe.

And then there's our changeless weather, that endless summer toward which our whole continent surfs dreaming to landfall on Muscle Beach in one great jumble-sale of sunburnt limbs.

Our endless summer.

That's how they got us wrong long long ago.

Describing L.A. as the laid-back, snooze-happy town.

Laid-back, no. Stand aside, yes.

To let you pass, let you go, let you become.

It only pretends to be cool. I hate cool people. Next thing you know they are cold. Soon after they rent rooms at Forest Lawn.

Not the real Angeleno.

We are in a state of Becoming. If we persist we will go on becoming whatever in hell it is we want to be.

So there you have it. Los Angeles is everything you want to be. Whatever you decide, L.A. becomes. It stands still. You move.

Your engine drives the machine. The machine isn't laid-back, nor is it LALA-Land encrypted. It only looks that way, waiting for you to tromp the gas and strike the spark.

You want to thrive in the foothills, linger at the beach, carouse Boyle Heights, pretend a half-life in Beverly Hills? Go!

The simple fact is there is no single, static Los Angeles. With luck, there never will be.

When Francois Truffaut, the French film director, first visited L.A. 35 years ago I sweated to plan what to show him. My wife and I finally trekked him out to the Valley's Piggly Wiggly Continental, one of the first supermarkets where you could buy all the things you didn't need. He ran amok like a child, seizing bright junk. We ended the night atop Mulholland Drive, where we showed him our City of Light, 500 square miles of lights extending from sea to (almost) Salton Sea.

◄ **HULA-HOOP HOPEFULS PRACTICE FOR A 1950s-STYLE CONTEST, STUDIO DRIVE-IN, LOS ANGELES**
AUGUST 1989
Fun, frolic, frivolity and fads have long been a part of life in Los Angeles.

DAY OF THE DEAD PARADE

NOVEMBER 1979

Día de los Muertos, or Day of the Dead, takes place on November 2, two days after Halloween. The centuries-old Latin American tradition is celebrated with offerings of flowers and other mementos to the departed and street parades that, while resembling funeral processions, are actually upbeat and joyful. This parade begins each year from Evergreen Cemetery in East Los Angeles.

"See all those lights," I said. Six million lights each representing an individual who doesn't have to join the pell-mell rush. Six million singles who don't have to "go fetch!" but turn in circles on their own Reebok deck shoes, watching the freeways fill with quasi–New Yorkers while they quietly manifest themselves on off-paths and side streets, managing to get where they want to go ahead of the crowd.

L.A. My town. A town with no elbows, no hustles. Where you pick your neighbors 10 miles off and ignore those across the fence if their shadow lies funny on your lawn.

A town of those endless summers with the ghosts of surfers nudging Malibu, daring the mudslide to bury them or the brushfire to torch them. Not laid-back but upright, hanging ten. A town more real than real and therefore a town worth dreaming in. A town where you can trade your surgically sculpted abs and ass for a stroller and playpen and not mind the change.

So here's to Los Angeles, diverse, multitudinous, going, arriving, a gigantic pinball device whose chartless dreams ricochet Tomorrow.

May it never be homogenized, may it never be described.

Ray Bradbury is the author of a large body of fiction, including The Martian Chronicles *and* Fahrenheit 451. *The longtime resident of Los Angeles has never learned to drive a car.*

INTRODUCTION

CARLA LAZZARESCHI

FROM ITS INCEPTION, LOS ANGELES HAS BEEN shaped by the urgent dreams of its people. The seemingly boundless and often impractical ambitions and appetites of the men and women who settled here propelled them to hope and dare on a grand scale, and to quite literally imagine a city into being. These were people for whom dreams and daring were both rudder and compass.

"Los Angeles has not grown; it has been conjured into existence," wrote Carey McWilliams more than 50 years ago in his seminal dissection of the region, *Southern California: An Island on the Land*.

At no time in its nearly 220-year history was that more clear than in the 20th century. As the century began, Los Angeles had neither a reliable water supply nor a useful natural harbor. There were no mineral or timber resources. Pinned among mountain chains, a punishing desert and an ocean, the region is subject to earthquakes, floods and wind-propelled fires. In short, with the exception of the mild climate and abundant sunshine, the fates had dealt the region a weak hand, offering little to suggest that this place could sustain intense urbanization, let alone evolve as it has.

Yet there were those whose vision said otherwise. They were mesmerized by the possible and undaunted by the improbable. Henry Huntington, the real estate tycoon who

created the Pacific Electric Railway and later endowed the library, museum and gardens that still bear his name, was one of them. "I believe that Los Angeles is destined to become the most important city in this country, if not the world," he said in 1920. Along with other like-minded and creative souls, he took steps to make it happen.

The largest city in the world to emerge during the last century, Los Angeles is perhaps the quintessential 20th-century metropolis. It did not merely grow dramatically during the last 10 decades—rather, it exploded, from a population of slightly more than 102,000 residents clustered on about 45 square miles in 1900 to nearly 4 million residents stretched across some 465 square miles at the

IMPORTING A PALM TREE
1888

Like its citizens, Los Angeles' palm trees are mostly imported. Thousands like this one were planted during the 1920s and 1930s. The only true native species is the towering California palm, which grows as high as 70 feet.

close of the century. Today the nation's second most populous city—only New York claims more residents—covers a territory roughly equal to the combined areas of St. Louis, Milwaukee, Cleveland, Minneapolis, Boston, San Francisco and Manhattan.

Along the way Los Angeles gave birth to, or put its own unique spin on, many of the most important innovations of the 20th century, from the movies to the automobile, from aviation to animation. Even the Internet, perhaps the most important creation of the final decades of the 20th century, lists UCLA as its spawning ground. Los Angeles also became home to immigrants from nearly all points on the globe, who have bestowed on the city an international flavor and rhythm that is unparalleled on the planet.

This collection of photos represents an attempt to tell the amazing story of what was created in Los Angeles during the 20th century by the people who settled here. Collected from archives throughout Southern California, these photos depict not only the culture that we made for ourselves, but the icons and attitudes that have become a part of the world's experience.

As the new century begins, Los Angeles continues to attract people propelled by urgent dreams. But as we idle on the freeways and cope with overcrowded schools, strained social services, scarce housing, endangered water supplies and overtaxed waste disposal services, we are paying the price for ambitions that succeeded beyond all imagining.

Population estimates tell us that California is gaining new residents at the rate of one every 51 seconds, a sizable percentage of them in Los Angeles. The population of the six-county region that comprises Southern California, already at 16.4 million, is expected to increase by 6 million within the first 20 years of the new millennium. Unlike a century ago, no urgent advertising campaigns and no Chamber of Commerce promotional railroad cars are required to lure the newcomers. They result from birth, immigration and the promise of a booming and diverse economy.

The urban builders of previous generations dreamed of expansion—of spreading the city out, filling it up, and building empires where nothing existed. The visionaries of today and tomorrow haven't much room left for that. Their talents will be required in conservation, restoration and recycling, in the innovative reuse of existing facilities, and in the difficult community work of ensuring that the bounty of what we have created can be shared in social harmony.

"More than any other city, the greatness of Los Angeles must be attributed to the ingenuity of its people," said Tom Bradley, the city's first African-American mayor and the man who guided it through its dramatic growth spurt in the 1970s and '80s. While Bradley no doubt was referring to 20th-century achievements, the city can take his words as a prescription for handling its challenges over the coming hundred years.

Whether the city's new century will be as astonishing as its last is the tale that remains to be told by all who live here, dreaming and acting, as each day passes, each picture is taken and each story unfolds.

CITRUS WORKERS WITH THE SAN GABRIEL MOUNTAINS IN BACKGROUND ▶
CIRCA 1935

This scene of a lush orange grove set against the snowcapped mountains became a signature view for the hundreds of thousands of acres of citrus under cultivation in Southern California. Countless Chambers of Commerce in the region used such scenes as a promotional device to draw both tourists and settlers, as well as to illustrate the glories and new opportunities of working as a gentleman farmer. Citrus labels, now collected as a beautiful art form, also helped to glamorize and popularize such scenes to a wide audience.

13

**FRAMING THE FIRST RESIDENTIAL TOWER
ATOP BUNKER HILL**

MAY 1968

All existing structures on a dozen blocks of downtown's Bunker Hill were cleared away, and office and residential towers, like this one, rose in their place during the Bunker Hill Redevelopment Project which completely transformed the area.

SETTING THE SCENE

A scant hundred years ago, it was obvious to some that,
in this basin of dust and brush, a world-class city could be built.

◀ **CONSTRUCTION OF THE PIPELINE USED TO TRANSPORT WATER FROM THE OWENS RIVER VALLEY**

CIRCA 1911

A spirit of willful self-determination has enabled Los Angeles to triumph repeatedly over daunting geographic limitations. That spirit was exemplified in the drive to bring vast quantities of water to this semiarid region to promote population growth and agriculture during the early 20th century. The Owens River in California's eastern Sierra Nevada was tapped as the city's first major source of imported water. The men who went after the water rights did so by any means necessary, creating a legacy of scandal and bitterness. It was eventually said of California and its water policy that "no other place has put as many people where they probably have no business being."

CONSTRUCTION CREWS TAKING A REST FROM WORK ON THE LOS ANGELES AQUEDUCT

JUNE 1911

The Los Angeles Aqueduct, which opened in 1913 and cost taxpayers $40 million, draws water from the Owens Valley entirely by gravity and siphon, without a single electric pump. Supervised by the city's chief water engineer, William Mulholland, its construction combined such modern methods as electric dredges and Caterpillar tractors with mule teams and men wielding picks and shovels. The aqueduct, the longest in the world at 233 miles, was considered an engineering wonder, and Mulholland was hailed as a genius. Along with the later-constructed California and Colorado aqueducts, the Los Angeles Aqueduct still serves as one of the three pipelines importing water into Southern California.

18

WATER IN LOS ANGELES AQUEDUCT
ON OPENING DAY

NOVEMBER 5, 1913

The official "uncorking" took place at the northern end of the San Fernando Valley, four miles north of the city of San Fernando near what is now Sylmar. Between 30,000 and 40,000 Angelenos attended—equivalent to about 10 percent of the city's population at the time. The city's banks printed free programs advising people to bring their own drinking cups. The ceremonies included song ("Hail the Water," sung by soprano Ellen Beach Yaw) and pageantry. William Mulholland unfurled an American flag and gave a short but eloquent speech praising the proponents of the aqueduct. An army regiment fired a cannon salute, several engineers turned the wheel, and people raced to the sides of the cascade to see the water rush down. Mulholland then turned to Mayor Henry Rose and, choked with emotion, uttered these now-famous words: "There it is. Take it."

**MULLHOLLAND DAM AND RESERVOIR
BENEATH HOLLYWOODLAND SIGN**

1926

Completed in 1924, the 200-foot-tall dam at the base of the Hollywood Reservoir has long been considered one of the most beautiful in America. Originally the dam was named after Los Angeles City Engineer William Mulholland. But following the catastrophic collapse in 1928 of the Mulholland-designed dam at San Francisquito, in which hundreds of lives were lost, the Hollywood dam was renamed to match the famous (and now four letters shorter) Hollywood sign under which it is nestled. Visible in the hills at the top center of the photo is a well-known estate owned at various times by gangster Bugsy Siegel and pop singer Madonna. The nine-level, 7,800-square-foot Mediterranean-style house, named Castillo del Lago (Castle of the Lake), was built in the 1920s to take advantage of the man-made lake view. The tree-lined three-mile path around the reservoir, which has supplied much of Los Angeles' domestic water for more than 75 years, remains a popular walking area for residents.

**LOS ANGELES RIVER CONSTRUCTION,
LOOKING NORTH FROM ATWATER VILLAGE**
1938
Many modern Angelenos are unaware that a 58-mile river cuts through the city, running from the foothills above the San Fernando Valley to the harbor at Long Beach. For more than a century, the Los Angeles River provided most of the city's drinking water and irrigated its vineyards and orange groves. But the river was volatile, and, after a catastrophic flood in 1938 killed 87 people and flooded 108,000 acres of Los Angeles County, construction began on

a constraining channel. Some consider the effort, which took 20 years and cost nearly $117 million, a "concrete coffin." Still, the river swells dramatically after winter rains, and storm runoff can reach a speed of 45 miles per hour as it races toward the Pacific Ocean at a descent rate steeper than that of even the mighty Mississippi.

LOS ANGELES HARBOR ▶
1926
The absence of a natural harbor was another daunting obstacle facing Los Angeles as it

battled toward its unlikely destiny as the largest city on the West Coast. To boost trade, industry and population growth, it became critical to create a man-made deep-water harbor. A 10-year battle—the Free Harbor Fight—ensued over whether to dredge the bay at Santa Monica or at San Pedro, 16 miles south. Collis P. Huntington, head of the powerful Southern Pacific Railroad, lobbied fiercely for Santa Monica, hoping to secure a shipping monopoly for his railroad. But government studies—and the powerful *Los Angeles Times*—favored San Pedro, which was finally

chosen. Dredging and construction began in 1899. In 1906, Los Angeles annexed the harbor area and a shoestring of land 16 miles long and a mere half-mile wide that would officially connect the city with the San Pedro site. A second harbor was later created at Long Beach, and the adjacent waterfronts now constitute the largest man-made harbor in the world. Once again Los Angeles thrived artificially by creating resources where they did not exist.

WATER AND OIL MIX AT HUNTINGTON BEACH, VIEWED FROM HUNTINGTON PIER

JANUARY 1940

Southern California's oil boom began in 1892 when prospector Edward Doheny correctly divined that natural pools of petroleum were buried beneath the city's bubbling tar pits. California quickly became the third largest oil-producing state in the nation. This dra-

matic photograph illustrates the aggressive pursuit of "black gold" after Huntington Beach became, in 1920, the site of one of the largest oil strikes ever in Southern California. The thicket of wells shown here remained part of the local landscape for decades. Less obtrusive oil pumps still operate in the Los Angeles basin. Even after 100 years, the region's oil fields have not been exhausted.

**WILSHIRE BOULEVARD BETWEEN FAIRFAX
AND LA BREA AVENUES**

CIRCA 1918

Known at the time of this photo as "El
Camino Viejo," or "Old Road," this sleepy section of unpaved roadway several miles west of
the thriving downtown community retained
its pastoral appearance for decades. But the

automobile was about to decentralize Los Angeles and change everything in its path. In the early 1920s, realtor A. W. Ross and developer H. Gaylord Wilshire transformed this section of the road into an upscale shopping district, catering to motorists rather than pedestrians and attracting such retailers as May Company, Silverwoods, Phelps-Terkel and Desmond's. Eventually ballyhooed as the city's "Miracle Mile" shopping district, the boulevard became a great center of capitalist commerce. Ironically, it was named for Wilshire, an affluent free thinker who ran for Congress, unsuccessfully, as a Socialist.

WORKMEN GRADE HOLLYWOOD BOULEVARD NEAR THE TURN OF THE CENTURY

1890s

This dirt road surrounded by farmland would become one of the city's grandest and glitziest boulevards within 30 years of this photo. The nearby steam train, used for earthmoving, presaged the passenger trolleys that would soon bring hopeful home buyers and speculators to land sales offices out in the "sticks," as these rural areas were then called, where huge returns would be promised on investments.

◀ RAILROAD PASSENGERS CROWD SANTA FE STATION IN LOS ANGELES

CIRCA 1910

When the Santa Fe Railroad initiated its service to Los Angeles in 1885, it offered a promotional fare of $8 from Kansas City to the coast. The previous charge, on competing Southern Pacific, had been $125. The crushing influx of passengers resulted in L.A.'s population boom of 1887. The Santa Fe also brought Los Angeles its first direct rail link to Chicago. This photo was taken at the Santa Fe's L.A. terminus, called La Grande Station, at Second Street and Santa Fe Avenue. The Moorish-style depot, which no longer stands, was built in 1893 for $50,000.

THE GREEN HOTEL, PASADENA

CIRCA 1910

The Green Hotel was among the grandest and busiest of the "boom hotels" constructed to house tourists and speculators brought in by the railroads. Rising up in what appeared to be the middle of nowhere, they offered newcomers a luxurious end-of-the-line experience designed to persuade them to stay on, and created an aura of prosperity meant to stimulate further investment. Built in Pasadena by patent-medicine king G. G. Green, the "Castle Green," as it's known, opened in January 1890 and hosted President Benjamin Harrison and his wife the following year. The west wing has since been converted to private housing units, and the east wing was demolished. The Hotel del Coronado in San Diego is another outstanding boom hotel from the 1880s.

RETURN DRIVE, ON LOOKOUT MOUNTAIN AT LAUREL CANYON, WITH THE LOOKOUT MOUNTAIN INN IN THE DISTANCE

CIRCA 1908

Real estate was the real gold in turn-of-the-century Los Angeles. Few who viewed this barren hillside then could have envisioned the transformation that would take place after several decades of piped-in water and population growth. Today Laurel Canyon is a lushly landscaped area of multimillion-dollar homes with glittering city views. This photograph of the Lookout Mountain Inn, a posh and popular tourist resort, was taken the year the area was first subdivided into view lots. Bungalows soon sprouted. A trackless electric trolley, built in 1912, ran every half-hour from Sunset Boulevard to the top of the mountain. A fire destroyed the inn in 1918.

GLENDALE SANITARIUM, GLENDALE

CIRCA 1900

From the 1870s to the turn of the century, health seekers suffering from tuberculosis, asthma and rheumatism flooded into Southern California, drawn by the mild, dry climate and low railroad fares. The Glendale Sanitari-um, built in 1887 and located near Sycamore Canyon, was operated by Seventh-day Adventists. It offered hydrotherapy, "phototherapy," thermotherapy, Swedish gymnastics, Turkish baths and special diets. Around 1900, doctors found that tuberculosis could be treated even in harsh East Coast climates, and the influx of health seekers began to wane. The Glendale Sanitarium later became a hotel and was torn down around 1924.

THIRD STREET LOOKING TOWARD HILL STREET
CIRCA 1898
A horse and buggy makes its way through peaceful streets lined with Victorian homes in turn-of-the-century Bunker Hill. The area was then a thriving residential enclave inhabited by well-to-do doctors, lawyers and mer-

chants, some of whom commuted to work by taking the short Angels Flight railway down the hill.

DOWNTOWN SPRING STREET,
LOOKING NORTH FROM SECOND STREET ▶
CIRCA 1895

Downtown Los Angeles had a strikingly European flavor at the turn of the century, with its busy street life offset by ornate hotel fronts and a skyline spiked with turrets and spires. At the center rises the clock tower of the original county courthouse, a spectacular, fortress-like structure of red sandstone, com-

pleted in 1891. It stood next to the old Hall of Records and housed the county jail. Like many landmark Los Angeles buildings, it was damaged in the 1933 Long Beach earthquake and was finally torn down in 1936.

GRIFFITH PARK, LOOKING SOUTHEAST, WITH GRIFFITH OBSERVATORY IN FOREGROUND

JANUARY 1936

By the mid-1930s, the once-barren hills of Los Feliz, Glendale and Hollywood had been transformed into thriving residential and retail areas, as seen in this view from Griffith Park. Griffith Observatory was brand new when this photo was taken. With its gleaming Classical Moderne–style dome and its spectacular views of both the night skies above and the city below, the facility was embraced by the public and continues to draw overflow crowds each weekend. Designed by John C. Austin, one of the architects of L.A.'s elegant City Hall, the building features interior murals done by Hugo Ballin, a WPA-era artist. The observatory became etched in cinema history in the 1955 movie *Rebel Without a Cause*, which starred James Dean; a bronze bust of the actor stands on the grounds.

CONSTRUCTION OF CITY HALL, LOS ANGELES ▶

1926

By the 1920s, Los Angeles cried out for a city hall worthy of its ambitions, and settled on this unusual upward-thrusting tower. The only building of its time allowed to rise above 150 feet (a limit imposed in the city due to earthquake danger), the 28-story tower with its classical temple base and Egyptian overtones was inspired by the work of the brilliant designer Bertram Goodhue. So symbolic was its role as the center of government in a city destined to dominate the state that city fathers decreed that the mortar used to construct it would consist of sand from each county in the state and water from each of the 21 Spanish missions. The tapering tower gained national prominence after being cast as the *Daily Planet* building in the *Superman* television series, and later as police headquarters in the *Dragnet* TV shows.

◀ UNION STATION INTERIOR
UNDER CONSTRUCTION
CIRCA 1938

The last great train station built in the United States, Union Station was completed in 1939 in a style quintessentially Southern Californian—a heady combination of Spanish Mission and Streamline Moderne. The gigantic station, mobbed by 1.5 million people in its first three days of operation, served the wartime passengers of the Santa Fe, Southern Pacific and Union Pacific railroads. It later fell into decline as a result of improved highways and air travel. In 1990 the Catellus Development Corporation purchased the 50-acre site and began renovation. The beautifully restored Union Station now serves Amtrak, the city's nascent Metro Rail subway and the Metrolink light rail system that runs between Los Angeles and its surrounding suburbs.

NIGHTTIME PERFORMANCE
AT THE HOLLYWOOD BOWL
JUNE 1960

Now the summer home of the Los Angeles Philharmonic, the Hollywood Bowl site was initially identified by H. Ellis Reed, who was enthralled by its amazing acoustics while hiking in Cahuenga Pass. The land was owned by Myra Hershey (of the Hershey Chocolate family), and she worked with Artie Mason Carter, Charles E. Toberman and others to develop the amphitheater. The first season opened in 1916 with a production of *Julius Caesar*, starring Tyrone Power Sr. and Douglas Fairbanks Sr. The acoustics were improved with a shell, designed by Lloyd Wright in 1924 and redesigned in 1928. The original shell has been replaced several times, most recently with a version by Frank O. Gehry in 1982. Summer concerts at the Bowl, which also features jazz, pop music and fireworks, are now an essential Los Angeles experience.

KNEELING WOMAN AT THE ENTRANCE TO THE HOLLYWOOD BOWL

CIRCA 1940

As prosperity and confidence took root in Los Angeles, so did the beginnings of an enduring cultural life. The Los Angeles Symphony was established in 1897, the first such orchestra west of the Rocky Mountains. It would eventually take up summer residence here at the Hollywood Bowl, a natural amphitheater. In the 1930s, the Bowl gained dramatic Art Deco–style entrance gates commissioned by the Depression-era Federal Arts Project. This figure, cast in concrete in 1935, is one of three large-scale decorative pieces by sculptor George Stanley. The kneeling woman, playing a harp, represents music; an 11-foot male symbolizes drama, and an 11-foot female symbolizes dance.

38

**RECENTLY COMPLETED SUBDIVISION
OF KAISER HOMES, IN NORTH HOLLYWOOD
AT THE BASE OF THE HOLLYWOOD HILLS**

FEBRUARY 1948

A seemingly endless stream of suburban neighborhoods, crisscrossed by wide commercial boulevards, is the most significant landscape feature of Los Angeles' outlying areas. Annexed by the city in 1915, the San Fernando Valley would make the dream of a single-family home and yard a reality for countless young families. A major housing boom began as World War II ended, fueled by federal loan programs and the G.I. Bill of Rights. Kaiser Homes, a neighborhood of 922 single-family residences, was completed in early 1948. By 1960 the population of the Valley had soared to 850,000, quintupling in less than 20 years. By 1970 its population was 1.8 million. Despite average housing costs among the highest in the nation, the American Dream has held fast in Los Angeles. By 1980 the city held more private residences per capita than any other large city in the world.

**LOOKING NORTHWEST TOWARD THE
INTERSECTION OF SUNSET BOULEVARD,
CAÑON DRIVE AND RODEO DRIVE,
BEVERLY HILLS**

1920s

The rich are different—you knew that, but you're reminded of it when you encounter the wide, curving boulevards of Beverly Hills. Designed by Wilbur Clark to converge at the landmark Beverly Hills Hotel, constructed in 1911–12, these palm-lined avenues offer an expansive sense of luxury and privacy, in striking contrast to the more prosaic grid of the Hollywood area. Their sweeping curves also make the nearby hills more visible. The fabled burg got its name when Burton E. Green, a real estate magnate from the East, acquired much of what had been a 4,500-acre rancho in 1907 and christened it in memory of his hometown of Beverly Farms, Massachusetts.

◀ **PARK LA BREA HOUSING COMPLEX, LOOKING NORTHEAST, WITH THE SAN GABRIEL MOUNTAINS IN THE DISTANCE**
1954

Even in the densely populated mid-Wilshire area of the central city, not far from downtown Los Angeles, this housing complex is one of the few vertical developments. The massive Park La Brea, with 4,253 living units, was designed to hold 10,000 residents. It was part of a plan for innovative urban villages developed by the Metropolitan Life Insurance Company prior to World War II. The first of these town homes opened in 1944. Sitting on 176 acres in the middle of Los Angeles, Park La Brea is still the largest apartment community west of the Mississippi. Its sister villages include Park Merced in San Francisco and Park Fairfax in Fairfax, Virginia, near Washington, D.C.

WATTS TOWERS, 107TH STREET IN WATTS
1969

Few landmarks speak more effectively of the Angeleno's determined struggle for self-expression, however eccentric, than Watts Towers. Constructed without means, plans or permit by an Italian immigrant, Simon Rodia, who labored at them for more than 30 years, the lacy, seemingly magical towers rise as high as 100 feet above a largely African-American neighborhood that has struggled with poverty and racism. A tileworker by trade, Rodia built the towers between 1921 and 1954, using discarded steel reinforced with chicken wire and cement. Alongside neighborhood children, he decorated them with found objects like pottery shards, glass, tile and bottle caps. Amazingly, the towers have survived earthquakes and structural tests to become an enduring landmark, and Rodia, who was 81 when he stopped working on his opus and retired to Northern California, is considered a significant folk artist.

◄ **IDLED BULLDOZERS WAIT OUT LEGAL SNARLS DURING DODGER STADIUM CONSTRUCTION**

1960

A major new feature of the Los Angeles landscape—a baseball stadium dedicated to the home team—took shape on the steep hills of Chavez Ravine, shown here freshly bulldozed in 1960. The Dodgers, recently imported from Brooklyn, were already playing at their temporary home across town, the Coliseum.

MODERN-DAY BUNKER HILL TAKING SHAPE

MAY 1966

Bunker Hill as we know it today is yet another example of Los Angeles imposing its will to completely transform a landscape. Some of the crumbling Victorians of the former residential district, long in decline, were dismantled and shipped to new locales, like Heritage Square in nearby Highland Park. Others were simply bulldozed to be replaced by gleaming new office towers. Here the 42-story Union Bank building is constructed.

ECHO PARK LAKE, LOOKING NORTH

1920

Echo Park, where gently rolling hills combine with lush palms and a scenic lake to create an exotic ambience ideally suited to the city's subtropical setting, is one of several dreamlike pockets of beauty within Los Angeles' urban core. In the 1920s Echo Park—it was then known as Edendale—was a bucolic, rural neighborhood with stately homes. It also became the setting for numerous comical Keystone Kops movies. The lake was created in the 1860s to serve as a reservoir catch basin. The park did indeed once create an "echo" effect for people speaking loudly in its vicinity, but that has been obliterated by later plantings. The park's distinctive red wooden bridge has existed since the 19th century.

46

ANGELENOS IN THEIR SUNDAY BEST ENJOY A GONDOLA RIDE ON THE ALDERBAREN CANAL, NOW MARKET STREET, VENICE

1908

Few American cities feature a neighborhood more exotic than the canals of seaside Venice, developed at the turn of the century by Abbott Kinney, the restless heir to a tobacco fortune. At his behest, 16 miles of canal were dredged, weeping willows and gum trees were planted, Italian villas were built, and gondolas and singing gondoliers were imported from old Venice. The area thrived for some years before stagnation and sanitation problems caused the city to decree that the canals be filled in. Some of the canals survive today in a smaller but lushly planted and charming residential area, home to ducks as well as boats and sidewalks.

THE GRAND LAGOON AND MIDWAY PLAISANCE AT VENICE

1911

Abbott Kinney envisioned his city of Venice as a serious cultural center, but alas, the tastes of the public ran to such simpler diversions as freak shows, camel rides and roller coasters. The main tourist attractions were located here at the Plaisance, which opened in 1905 and featured performances by the Chicago Symphony Orchestra and actress Sarah Bernhardt. Eventually Kinney added a gargantuan dance hall and the world's largest indoor saltwater pool, and appealed to children with a huge Ferris wheel and a miniature train. The Venice area added a gay, bohemian flavor to life in growing Los Angeles. After years of decline and the loss of much of its distinctive Italianate architecture, the area is enjoying a comeback, but the Grand Lagoon shown here no longer exists, filled in to become what is now a traffic circle.

◀ **SURF CREEPING TOWARD HOUSES BUILT ON PILINGS AT TOPANGA BEACH NEAR TUNA CANYON**

OCTOBER 1961

Expanding, expanding, expanding, Los Angeles pushed all the way to the edge. Homesites right above the ocean surf were among the most desirable and sought after, in spite of winter storms that sometimes destroyed them. Residents persisted, lured by ocean breezes and the singular lifestyle at the water's edge. After all, as state librarian Kevin Starr wrote, "Disaster is not an enduring discomfort—cold weather is an enduring discomfort."

HILLSIDE HOMES ON HINES DRIVE IN LOS ANGELES, SUPPORTED BY STILTS

MAY 1971

The empty fields, orange groves and vineyards of the 1920s gave way, over the course of 50 years, to a city so densely populated that developers have grown ever more resourceful in finding new places to build. These houses built on stilts in the Glassell Park neighborhood appear to be easy marks for the next big earthquake. Temblors occur as frequently as 30 times a day in Southern California, but virtually all are imperceptible.

50

SUNSET ON THE FORMER HUNTINGTON PALISADES BEACH, SANTA MONICA
CIRCA 1919

No deed of ownership is needed for Angelenos to enjoy the spiritual balm of a sunset, an invitation for private contemplation open to one and all. The area's richly colorful sunsets, which ironically are enhanced by air-polluting agents, beckon nightly to those in need of solace or inspiration. Many choose to watch from the railings in Palisades Park, above this beach where a lighthouse once stood.

HENRY E. HUNTINGTON OUTSIDE FRONT DOOR OF RESIDENCE IN SAN MARINO

1920

Huntington was the man behind the Red Car trolley line, the vast and popular system of public transportation that Angelenos enjoyed earlier this century. Huntington founded the Pacific Electric Railway Co., which operated the Red Cars. He was also among the largest landowners in Southern California. Interestingly, the Red Cars helped increase the value of far-flung tracts of land by allowing developers to expand the suburbs. Along with Harry Chandler, Huntington was also part of the syndicate that controlled much of the San Fernando Valley land that shot up in value after Mulholland's aqueduct was approved. Huntington's wealth had come originally from the Southern Pacific Railroad, founded by his uncle Collis. Modern Angelenos know Huntington chiefly through his cultural legacy, the Huntington Library, Art Collections and Botanical Gardens, open to the public at his former residence in San Marino. It houses the world-class book and manuscript collection to which Huntington devoted his retirement years.

DOROTHY BUFFUM CHANDLER WITH COUNTY SUPERVISORS AT MUSIC CENTER DEDICATION
SEPTEMBER 27, 1964

Powerful civic insider and booster Dorothy Chandler, center, became one of the most effective culture mavens in the city's history when she spearheaded a 10-year fund drive, from 1954 to 1964, to establish the Music Center. Besides sparking major contributions from wealthy Angelenos, including namesake donors Mark Taper and Howard Ahmanson, she involved the public in a campaign involving "buck bags," in which even contributions of a dollar were made to seem meaningful. Walt Disney designed the bags, in which volunteers collected $2.2 million, leading Disney to comment that "it truly is the people's Music Center." Mrs. Chandler, or "Buffy," a nickname taken from her maiden name, was also instrumental in saving the Hollywood Bowl from financial disaster in 1951. Born into the Long Beach family that owned Buffums department store, she married Norman Chandler, eldest son of *Los Angeles Times* publisher Harry Chandler, and frequently brought her influence to bear on the paper's editorial positions. Mrs. Chandler is surrounded by, from left: L.A. County Supervisors Kenneth Hahn, Warren Dorn, Frank Bonelli and Ernest Debs.

WALT DISNEY WAVES FROM THE CAB OF HIS TRAIN, THE "VIEWLINER," AT DISNEYLAND IN ANAHEIM

JUNE 1957

In 1955 Walt Disney helped put Southern California on the world map as a tourist destination when he opened his Disneyland theme park in Anaheim, an hour south of Los Angeles. His influence on the region began much earlier, however, with his groundbreaking efforts in animation. After creating influential shorts like *Steamboat Willie* and the first full-length animated feature, *Snow White and the Seven Dwarfs* (1938), Disney moved his animation studios in 1940 from the SilverLake area of Los Angeles to Burbank, employing a generation of animators who would help shape the industry. Aside from a worldwide entertainment conglomerate that includes the Disney movie and television studios in Burbank, Walt's immense legacy provides major funding for the California Institute of the Arts in Valencia, where many of today's animators are educated.

JOHN ANSON FORD

NOVEMBER 1957

A progressive force on the Los Angeles County Board of Supervisors from 1934 to 1958, John Anson Ford earned an unequaled reputation for integrity, fairness and concern for human rights. In 1943, at a time when Japanese Americans had been shipped off to wartime detention camps, Latinos had been attacked by U.S. servicemen in the explosive "Zoot Suit" riots and blacks were suffering police discrimination, Ford founded the County Human Relations Commission, which first explored ways to better the city's race relations. "With its hodgepodge of all different kinds of people," said Ford, "Los Angeles can exert a powerful influence for better relations between cultures and races." In 1937, when corruption in city government was at its worst, Ford ran for mayor in an unsuccessful bid to unseat incumbent Frank Shaw. In 1958 he was the first chairman of the State Fair Employment Practices Commission. He also helped change a law that had prevented the county from subsidizing cultural events. His long support of the arts was recognized in 1978 when the Pilgrimage Theater, an outdoor arena in the Cahuenga Pass, was renamed the John Anson Ford Theater.

TOM BRADLEY

SEPTEMBER 1986

During four consecutive terms as mayor from 1973 to 1993, Tom Bradley helped usher Los Angeles into the modern era as a world-class city. He envisioned Los Angeles as "the gateway to the Pacific Rim," with a thriving, modern downtown and a rapid-transit subway.

After wresting leadership of the troubled metropolis away from his flamboyant predecessor, Sam Yorty, Bradley set out to reform the police department, initiate low-income housing projects and launch a mass transit network. The city's first African-American mayor and a remarkable coalition builder, Bradley helped strengthen the economy and

counted the successful 1984 Summer Olympics as his greatest triumph. His greatest disappointment no doubt was his inability to prevent the racially charged riots in 1992. A Democrat, he ran twice for governor of California but lost each time to Republican George Deukmejian.

GOLD PANNING IN SAN GABRIEL CANYON
APRIL 1935

Countless new settlers came to the Los Angeles area believing they could strike it rich, one way or another. Inevitably, some were disappointed. It's little known that California's first gold strike actually was in Southern California—about 40 miles northwest of Los Angeles, at a place then called San Francisquito, in March 1842. The mines there yielded the first gold sent from California to the U.S. mint at Philadelphia, and lured prospectors north from Sonora, Mexico. In 1848 a much richer strike at Sutter's Mill in Northern California captured the imagination of the public and sparked the great California gold rush. In this photo, the faithful pan for gold flakes.

CASTING CALL AT PARAMOUNT PICTURES, BRONSON GATE

1930

The motion picture industry has attracted far more people to Southern California than it has ever employed. Still, from 1920 to 1940 the movies were the leading industry in Los Angeles. In 1939 the industry employed 30,000 to 40,000 workers and spent $190 million on film production, most of it for salaries and wages. The movie industry made a good fit with the city of Los Angeles—both were based on improvisation, make-believe and good weather. In this photograph from 1930, hopefuls gather for a casting call at the gates of Paramount Pictures, the only major studio still located in Hollywood. According to studio lore, it was under this arch that Gloria Swanson as Norma Desmond uttered the immortal line, "I'm ready for my close-up now, Mr. DeMille."

62

**EXERCISE GURU PAUL BRAGG LEADS
SHOULDER-TOUCHES FOR A GROUP OF
OUTDOOR ENTHUSIASTS, HOLLYWOOD HILLS**
1929

The siren call of good health drew countless thousands to this warm, dry region, especially in the years 1890–1910, when tuberculosis swept the country. As the city grew up, even the healthy found themselves immersed in a culture where athletics and physical well-being often took center stage. A cult of the body and of the out-of-doors took hold in Southern California long before most Americans had ever encountered a "workout" beyond those in a high school gym. Paul Bragg, shown here, was a nutritionist who lectured on the evils of sugar and other health-related topics. He is said to have inspired Joe DiMaggio, then a sickly child of 15, to become fit. Bragg led exercise groups on hikes through the Hollywood Hills. Here a group of outdoors enthusiasts is shown alongside Fern Dell, just north of Los Feliz Boulevard.

**CHAMBER OF COMMERCE SCENE PROMOTING
VIRTUES OF COMBINING BUSINESS
AND PLEASURE IN SOUTHERN CALIFORNIA ▶**
1930s

"We've Got the Climate for Business," boasted the Chamber in its caption for this photograph, touting glorious beach weather and a "wide-awake" business community, and rather presciently envisioning an era when cell phones and laptop computers would make doing business at the beach almost commonplace.

CHILDREN WALK BETWEEN TENTS IN CAMP MEETING OF SEVENTH-DAY ADVENTISTS

1938

Camp meetings were a popular practice among Seventh-day Adventists, back as far as 1842, when the open-air gatherings were originated to promote Bible study, fellowship and interest in the Advent, or second coming of Christ, which followers at that time believed would occur in 1843. A wide variety of religions took hold in the Los Angeles area, partly because the frontier nature of the city bred openness and tolerance, and partly because a significant number of new residents arrived suffering serious health maladies and sought spiritual solace during what they feared might be their final days. The area's bizarre cults and sects drew the most publicity, but the majority of residents pursued a more traditional, fundamentalist path. Protestantism was the city's dominant religion in its formative years.

**AIMEE SEMPLE McPHERSON ADDRESSING
A THRONG OF CHILDREN IN FRONT OF HER
HOME ADJOINING ANGELUS TEMPLE**

JUNE 1926

Evangelist Aimee Semple McPherson emerged as something of a messiah to the spiritually hungry hordes in the Los Angeles of the 1920s.

With a gift for preaching and a flair for showmanship, she built her Foursquare Gospel church into a powerhouse with nationwide influence. Five years after arriving in town with $100 in her pocket, she was able to build the showplace 5,300-seat Angelus Temple, which still overlooks Echo Park. Her daily broadcasts on radio station KFSG extended her reach far beyond the lakefront church. The vaudeville-style antics she led on the stage of her Temple were dubbed "the best in town" by no less a showman than Charlie Chaplin. But Aimee's immense popularity irritated the city's Protestant establishment. When a "kidnapping" episode in which she was missing for 36 days began to smell like a publicity stunt, the district attorney's office went after her on morals charges, claiming she'd really been away with a lover. Though charges were dropped, Aimee's ministry never quite recovered its momentum.

CITRUS PACKERS GRADING ORANGES
FOR SIZE AND QUALITY, COLLEGE HEIGHTS
ORANGE ASSOCIATION, CLAREMONT

AUGUST 1935

If fortunes from gold or Hollywood proved elusive, newcomers might turn to oranges, the gold that grew in groves encircling the region. The citrus industry attracted fully as many people to California as did the gold rush, with a far more reliable yield—and one that would vastly exceed the value of gold produced in the state. Thousands of jobs were created, and many fortunes made. The California Fruit Growers Association, a cooperative that adopted the trade name Sunkist, at one point controlled 70 percent of California's citrus crop. Chinese, Japanese and Mexican immigrants performed much of the labor. Early attempts to organize were brutally suppressed, particularly in the 1930s, when this photo was taken. Workers packing Athlete brand oranges in this photo were part of the Sunkist co-op.

**WOMEN AT WORK ON THE ASSEMBLY LINE
AT DOUGLAS AIRCRAFT'S LONG BEACH PLANT**
1941

Suffering a severe labor shortage during the war years, the aircraft industry opened its doors to women. By 1943, 40 percent of the industry's Los Angeles labor force was female. A study by Douglas ranked women's produc- tivity within 5 percent of men's, a strong showing given their relative lack of experi- ence. Even so, management's attitude could be patronizing. "We tell women to take it easy," said one foreman, "to imagine they are in the kitchen, baking a cake or washing dish- es." Vultee Aircraft published a study show- ing that the company lost $250 in productivi- ty every time a woman walked through the plant, because the men turned to look. Despite the apparent handicap, the defense industry in Los Angeles was the largest and most productive in the nation. In 1941, when this photo was taken, aircraft workers in the city filled orders worth a total of $550 million.

MEXICAN TORTILLA MAKERS AT THE EL SOL DEL MAYO FACTORY, 110 N. SPRING STREET
CIRCA 1930

Founded by settlers from Mexico in 1781, the city of Los Angeles has retained its Mexican character. In the early decades of this century, thousands of Mexicans were imported by railroad to work in the citrus industry and other enterprises. Many settled in Southern California and became the backbone of the migratory labor pool on which the state's agricultural harvest depended. Here, Mexican women hand-shape tortillas at downtown's El Sol Del Mayo factory, which was operated by Maria Quevedo during the first half of the century.

**MEN WORKING ON AN AIRCRAFT
ASSEMBLY LINE, BURBANK**

CIRCA 1930

Skilled carpenters were in demand at a time when aircraft were made of wood. Here, workers assemble the wooden fuselages of Vega monoplanes at a Lockheed facility. An abundance of open, flat land and a mild climate that allowed for outdoor assembly and maintenance of planes helped the aircraft industry thrive in Southern California, even before the war years brought in government contracts.

◄ **POTENTIAL BUYERS LINE UP TO VIEW AND PURCHASE LOTS FOR BEVERLYWOOD**

LATE 1930s

As civic boosterism succeeded and a new population poured in, Los Angeles speculators enjoyed mind-boggling profits during successive waves of cresting real estate booms. In two years in the 1920s, 1,400 new tracts were opened in Los Angeles County. Red and yellow flags waved over new acreage, and fantastic advertising helped quicken the pulses of potential buyers. Beverlywood, a residential community five minutes south of the Beverly Hills Hotel, was billed as the "Switzerland of Los Angeles," a refreshingly cool retreat from the heat elsewhere in the city, and homesites fetched between $2,000 and $4,000. Here, potential buyers line up to invest in lots that they were advised, not erroneously, could one day earn them "one hundred percent to one thousand percent" on their money.

CUSTOMERS THRONG THE OPENING DAY OF MAY CO.'S NEW APPLIANCE DEPARTMENT

JUNE 1946

The American Dream was within reach and needed furnishing for thousands of new homeowners in the postwar years. A suburbia that stretched as far as the eye could see was springing up in the San Fernando Valley, and a new prosperity put many modern conveniences on the shopping list.

72

RAY CORENSON (FRONT ROW, SECOND FROM RIGHT), THE "MOTHER OF THE HOME," LEADS PREPARATION OF FOOD AT THE LOS ANGELES JEWISH HOME FOR THE AGING IN BOYLE HEIGHTS

1929

New immigrants to Los Angeles often developed a pattern of settling into communities defined by race, religion or place of origin. By the 1920s, a substantial Jewish community existed in Boyle Heights, just east of downtown. Brooklyn Avenue was a real Jewish neighborhood, with Yiddish newspapers and kosher butcher shops. Centers like the Jewish Home for the Aging helped maintain tradition and community. In subsequent decades, more affluent Jewish communities took root in the Fairfax area, near the Wilshire district and in Beverly Hills. By the early 1980s, Los Angeles was home to more than 600,000 Jews—the world's third largest Jewish city, after New York and Tel Aviv. Jews became highly influential in the movie industry, the apparel and building industries, the retail and wholesale trades, and the professions.

**IOWANS CELEBRATE THEIR HOME STATE
AT AN IOWA DAY BARBECUE IN SOUTHERN
CALIFORNIA**

JULY 1924

The homing instinct was powerful in a city where, by 1930, nearly nine out of 10 people were relative newcomers. The so-called "state societies" were hugely successful, partly because they helped offset an acute loneliness that haunted the region. "They liquidate the blues," said C. H. Parsons, an Iowan who in 1909 led the formation of the Federation of State Societies in Los Angeles. The Iowans were the first to establish picnic meetings. The first Iowa Day picnic, held on a sunny January day in Pasadena in 1900, attracted 3,000 celebrants from the farm state. By the 1920s, when the event had moved to Bixby Park in Long Beach, it was drawing 150,000 Iowans annually. On Iowa Day, wrote Parsons, "a singular excitement was in the air, when, from far and near, the tribes begin to assemble." Eventually former Iowans would come from all over the world to attend state picnics in Southern California.

JAPANESE AMERICAN GIRLS
LINE A PARADE ROUTE

CIRCA 1929

Little Tokyo, around First and San Pedro streets downtown, thrived after the Japanese Association of America urged all Japanese to patronize only stores owned by other Japanese. By 1910 Los Angeles had more Japanese residents than any U.S. city except San Francisco. And by 1920, half the city's nonwhite population was Japanese. Agriculture and truck farming were the primary livelihoods of these new residents. During the early 1930s it was estimated that 90 percent of the produce consumed in Los Angeles was raised by Japanese farmers. The Japanese helped pioneer the West Coast fishing industry as well, and many also worked as gardeners and landscapers. Today the Asian community in Los Angeles includes enclaves of Chinese, Koreans, Filipinos, Samoans and Vietnamese, among others.

YOUNG BOYS OF CHAVEZ RAVINE ▶

CIRCA 1935

The Mexican population in Southern California increased after the turn of the century, with many new residents imported by train at the behest of business interests seeking labor for railroads, agriculture and industrial concerns. Like other ethnic groups, they tended to settle in homogeneous communities. One of these was Chavez Ravine, a working-class barrio in a steep canyon northeast of downtown, named for Julian Chavez, a member of the first Los Angeles City Council in 1850. In the 1950s, when the city decided to build a baseball stadium on the site for the transplanted Brooklyn Dodgers, 20 families who were longtime residents chose to resist the buyout. After much turmoil and publicity, they were finally evicted from their homes. The ravine is now the site of Dodger Stadium.

MARIACHIS ON THEIR WAY TO WORK IN EAST LOS ANGELES WALK PAST MURAL DEPICTING TRADITIONS IN MEXICAN MUSIC

JUNE 1985

Los Angeles is enriched by the presence of Mexican culture through language, food, public celebrations, mariachi and salsa music, murals and religious observances. Cinco de Mayo, which celebrates the Mexican defeat of French colonial forces at Puebla in 1861, is a major event here. Musicians customarily gather at Mariachi Plaza, on First Street near Boyle Heights, to await gigs. More than 3 million people of Mexican origin resided in Los Angeles County by the early 1990s.

CONGREGANTS GATHER IN FRONT OF THE FIRST AFRICAN METHODIST EPISCOPAL CHURCH ▶

JUNE 1942

The black community in Los Angeles experienced a political awakening after the turn of the century. Jefferson Lewis Edmond and others at the First AME Church, shown at right, created the Los Angeles Forum to foster political debate. John Somerville and his wife, Vada, the first two black graduates of USC's School of Dentistry, started a chapter of the NAACP. By 1930 Los Angeles was home to more than 20,000 African Americans, the largest black community on the Pacific Coast. Central Avenue, with its churches, businesses, nightspots and black-owned hotel, the Dunbar, was "Main Street" for black Los Angeles in the 1920s and '30s. The West Adams district, or "Sugar Hill," was also home to a growing black middle class. The war years brought steady work and new prosperity to many blacks as a labor shortage opened up jobs in the aircraft and defense industries and drew new migration from the South. Though they faced discrimination, especially via restrictive housing covenants, many families owned their own homes and operated churches, restaurants, businesses and nightclubs. By 1950, 218,000 blacks resided in Los Angeles County.

◄ SUMMERTIME CROWD JAMS VENICE BEACH

JULY 4, 1926

This Fourth of July crowd at Venice was the beach's largest yet. The strand was often crowded on weekends in the '20s, when one Red Car after another arrived throughout the day to deposit fun-seekers on the sand. The so-called Venice Short Line, which ran from downtown's Hill Street to Venice Beach in 50 minutes, was the most popular and profitable trip in the entire Pacific Electric system. Today crowds like this are seldom seen, as the automobile allows sun worshipers to find a spot almost anywhere along the beach.

WARDEN EXPLAINS THE RULES OF GRUNION CATCHING TO BEACH PARTY

1937

One of the odder traditions in Southern California life, the grunion run involves late-night forays to the beach during spring months to stalk the shiny, silvery fish that spawn on the sand under a full moon. The grunion ride the waves ashore, and the female deposits her eggs in a hole in the sand that she creates by swishing her tail. The male immediately fertilizes the eggs, and the fish then catch the next wave out to sea—unless they're snatched up by bare-handed beachgoers, who fry them on open campfires. Only a small percentage of the fish is affected, as the use of nets is prohibited.

◄ **BODY-BUILDERS PERFORM FOR
LABEL DAY CROWD AT MUSCLE BEACH**

SEPTEMBER 1954

L.A.'s cult of the body found its best expression at Muscle Beach, an area of Santa Monica devoted to body-building and gymnastics activities that took place right on the sand, just south of the pier, from 1934 to 1958. Joe Gold, Jack LaLanne and Steve "Hercules" Reeves strutted their stuff here; the site also

hosted the Mr. America and Mr. Universe contests. Huge crowds of spectators typically gathered, until annoyed merchants prompted the city to chase the body-builders away. The action was transplanted to Venice Beach, several miles down the strand, where the body-building scene thrived in the late '70s, when Arnold Schwarzenegger and others trained at Gold's Gym nearby. In 1999 the city installed new gymnastics equipment in Santa Monica,

on the site of the original Muscle Beach, and encouraged the weight lifters to return as part of a beachfront revitalization effort.

**EARLY SPORT-DIVING RIGS ARE TESTED
AT THE BEACH**

CIRCA 1933

Tire pumps create an offbeat air supply for these pioneering sport divers, who wear helmets made of hot water heaters modified

with viewing ports. Inventive approaches to water sports were typical of Southern California in its early days. Surfing, a major pursuit, was introduced here in 1907 from Hawaii but became far more popular in the 1950s, after Caltech designer Bob Simmons developed a lightweight synthetic board.

**LOS ANGELES DODGERS INAUGURAL GAME
AT THE COLISEUM**

APRIL 18, 1958

Luring the Dodgers from Brooklyn to Los
Angeles was a major coup for the city in 1958.

In earlier years, the West Coast was deemed
too far away to fit into the major league game
schedule, but the increased speed and range
of airplane flights made expansion feasible.
The Dodgers were promised a brand new

stadium in Chavez Ravine, but during its four-year construction they played at the Coliseum. A huge crowd of 78,672 turned out for their inaugural game, in which they beat 6-5 the other newly transplanted New York team, the San Francisco Giants. The Los Angeles Dodgers won the World Series the following year and went on to win it four more times, in 1963, 1965, 1981 and 1988.

ROSE PARADE WINNING ENTRY, PASADENA

JANUARY 1895

The Rose Parade started on New Year's Day 1890 as a promotional gimmick to lure people to Southern California by showcasing sunshine, oranges and flowers in the dead of winter. Pasadena was then a resort town of 4,000, and the first parade was quite a success, drawing 2,000 spectators to see buggies decorated with rose and orange blossoms, such as the one pictured above from the parade five years later. The Rose Bowl was built in 1922, and football became an official part of the festivities, with USC trouncing Penn State that year, 14-3.

THE KOMICAL KNIGHTS OF THE KARNIVAL, PASADENA

1911

This spiritual precursor to Pasadena's annual Doo Dah Parade took place for only two years, in 1911 and 1912, making good fun of the Rose Parade and L.A. in general, with floats like "12 Hours to Sixth and Main," which spoofed rapid transit, and another that featured suffragettes waving banners while their husbands did dishes and other household chores. Since 1978 the Doo Dah Parade has picked up the irreverent tradition, offering inspired silliness such as the Briefcase Drill Team and the West Hollywood cheerleaders, who sport flip skirts, wigs and five o'clock shadows. The Doo Dah parade takes place in Pasadena the weekend before Thanksgiving and draws about 30,000 onlookers.

SEBASTIAN'S COTTON CLUB IN CULVER CITY
1920s

Located "in the heart of screenland" near MGM studios, Frank Sebastian's Cotton Club advertised "plantation melodies, jazz, dancing and dining, with entertainment furnished by real Southern colored entertainers." At one point the stage featured the great jazz pianist and singer Lionel Hampton, shown above showcased with saxophonist Leon Herriford. Both had played with Louis Armstrong, who made his first Los Angeles appearance at Sebastian's. Greater Los Angeles, including Central Avenue, had a lively jazz scene earlier in this century. Swing was also born here, when Benny Goodman's orchestra and his rocking arrangements caused a sensation at the Palomar Ballroom in Los Angeles in 1935.

**NIGHTLIFE ON THE COAST
AS DONE AT THE COCOANUT GROVE
IN THE AMBASSADOR HOTEL**
CIRCA 1930

In the 1930s the nocturnal playgrounds that set the pace for glamorous L.A. nightlife sprang up mostly in Hollywood, along Sunset and Hollywood boulevards. Located farther south, on Wilshire Boulevard across from the original Brown Derby, was the grandest of them all, the capacious Cocoanut Grove at the Ambassador Hotel, which held more than a thousand people for dining and dancing and hosted lavish parties under its exotic indoor palm trees. Tragically, in 1968 the Ambassador was the scene of Robert Kennedy's assassination after he won the Democratic primary. The beautiful building, open since New Year's Eve 1921, finally closed its doors in 1990.

GANGSTER MICKEY COHEN TAKES A GOOD LOOK AT HIMSELF IN A WASHROOM MIRROR
CIRCA 1945

The underworld of Los Angeles sold plenty of newspapers in the heyday of the local press and has long fascinated the readers of crime novelists such as Raymond Chandler and James M. Cain. More recently it inspired James Ellroy's *L.A. Confidential*, which described the police corruption and racism of the 1930s and '40s as well as real-life figures like gangster Mickey Cohen. A former prizefighter and nightclub owner, Cohen took control of the Mob in Los Angeles when Benjamin "Bugsy" Siegel moved to Las Vegas in 1945. Cohen's violent battles with rival gangsters over the city's loan-sharking and gambling rackets came to be known as the "Sunset Wars," as bullets sometimes flew at Cohen's Sunset Boulevard haberdashery, a front for bookmaking. After spending considerable time in prison for tax evasion, Cohen died of cancer in 1976.

**LOS ANGELES POLICE DEPARTMENT
DRILL TEAM AT SECOND AND OLIVE STREETS,
LED BY LT. JOHN SNYDER**

JULY 1938

Forging a new public image was important for the LAPD in 1938, after reform mayor Fletcher Bowron took office and attempted to transform the police from a "frontier town" mentality to a more professional operation. Still, life on the force in the 1930s was rough. "Two-Gun" Jim Davis, the chief of police and a crack shot, reputedly used to invite residents in Echo Park to watch him shoot a cigarette out of the mouth of a young officer.

◀ **LOS ANGELES COUNTY DEPUTY SHERIFF WALTER HUNTER DESTROYS ILLEGAL SLOT MACHINES**

1938

Gambling came in and out of favor with the authorities in the 1920s and '30s, depending on whether local law enforcement was in a corrupt or reform phase. This photograph was taken in 1938 after Mayor Fletcher Bowron had been elected to clean up the city. County sheriffs confiscated a total of 17 slot machines during this raid. At other times the police and sheriffs condoned and even promoted bookmaking, gambling and other crimes, including prostitution and flagrant violations of Prohibition.

LOS ANGELES COUNTY SHERIFF PETER J. PITCHESS "CUTTING" THE RIBBON WITH A LIVE ROUND AT OPENING OF THE NEW PISTOL RANGE AT SHERIFF'S ACADEMY

APRIL 8, 1960

Pitchess severs the ribbon with a live round in a novel twist on an otherwise predictable event. Though harmless, the gesture suggest-ed the trigger-happy culture of local law enforcement, which has often been charged with overzealous use of force. Pitchess him-self was a former FBI agent who became known locally as a tough but professional taskmaster. His lengthy term as county sheriff ran from December 1958 to January 1982. He died in early 1999 at age 87.

ZOOT SUIT ARRESTEES, INGLEWOOD

1943

The topsy-turvy justice and racial tension of 1940s Los Angeles was reflected in the so-called Zoot Suit Riots. Random scuffles on the street between idle sailors and youthful Mexican Americans boiled over into a series of organized attacks and full-blown rioting in the summer of 1943, when military personnel from the Army, Navy and Marine Corps invaded Eastside barrios and assaulted young Latino men at will. On the worst night of the violence, June 7, several thousand servicemen and civilians swarmed over the central city, dragging pachucos into the street, stripping them and beating them. Police arrested the badly mauled victims rather than the perpetrators. Some press and local authorities opined that the soldiers were performing a service by cleaning up what was generally perceived as a bad element. The incidents took their name from the "zoot suit" clothing popular among Latinos at the time: draped pants with narrow cuffs; long, wide-shouldered jackets; and, usually, a hat and knee-length key chain.

JAPANESE-AMERICAN RESIDENTS REMOVED FROM THEIR HOMES ON VERMONT AVENUE DURING WORLD WAR II

FEBRUARY 1942

More than 34,000 Japanese Americans were removed from Los Angeles County during the war—considerably more than from any other community in the nation. Most spent the war years behind barbed wire, primarily at Manzanar in the Owens Valley, and at Heart Mountain, Wyoming. Many lost all of the belongings and land they had left behind. The action was taken in the name of national security under Executive Order 9066, a presidential decree affecting all Japanese nationals and U.S. citizens of Japanese descent. Not a single instance of sabotage by either group was ever verified. Japanese-American soldiers fought valiantly for the U.S. during World War II, winning more Medals of Honor than any other minority group. Congress acknowledged the injustice in 1988 and approved reparations for Japanese Americans. Payments began in 1990.

TONY'S SHOESHINE STAND, SOUTH LOS ANGELES, FOLLOWING WATTS RIOTS

AUGUST 1965

This resilient resident gets back to business after the Watts Riots, which caused $40 million in damage and destroyed both black- and white-owned businesses in an 11-square-mile area of Los Angeles over six days of rioting. More than 1,000 people were injured, and 34 died. Although triggered by a scuffle following the arrest of a young black motorist for drunk driving by the California Highway Patrol, the ensuing six days of looting, burning and killing were fueled by a deterioration in local living conditions and tenuous relations with the police. Part of a wave of national anger and dissatisfaction in the 1960s, the riots had counterparts in Chicago and Washington, D.C., in 1968 and 1969, and in other smaller flashpoints across the country.

VOLUNTEERS CLEAN UP ON HOOVER STREET NEAR KOREATOWN EVEN AS RIOTS CONTINUE
MAY 1992

Los Angelenos who believed that race relations had settled into a state of benign acceptance got a rude shock in 1992, when the city erupted after four white Los Angeles police officers were acquitted in the beating of black motorist Rodney King. A wide swath of the city suffered seven days of fires, vandalism and looting that left 51 dead, more than 2,000 injured, and damages of more than $500 million. But even as rioters in other parts of the city continued their destruction, thousands of volunteers emerged to remove the rubble and debris. Armed with shovels, brooms and pitchforks and fueled from a vast commissary of donated sandwiches, volunteers prayed, sang, swept and scrubbed together in an act of civic healing and cleansing.

**CHILDREN ABOARD OFFICER'S MOTORCYCLE
DURING FIRST WATTS FESTIVAL**

AUGUST 1966

Los Angeles police officer Gil Lout turns his bike over to a crew of apprentice riders during the Watts Festival, inaugurated a scant year after the Watts Riots to improve community relations. A tribute to the 34 people who died in the 1965 civil disturbances, the festival has become a community tradition that continues to this day. Past festivals have attracted tens of thousands of participants. Bill Cosby and Coretta Scott King, the widow of civil rights leader Martin Luther King Jr., are among those who have served as grand marshals of the festival parade.

**FORMER GANG MEMBERS PASTE UP
AN ANTI-GANG POSTER ON WALL ALONG
VERMONT AVENUE**

JANUARY 1989

After decades of gang warfare in Los Angeles that intensified in the 1980s, ending the lives of innocent children and neighbors as well as hundreds of young men every year, communities tried recruiting former gang members like these to help spread a message of reconciliation and healing. But change didn't come easily; in 1990, the year after this photo was taken, law enforcement tallied 650 gang-related homicides, up from 554 a year earlier. In the aftermath of the 1992 riots, the two largest African-American gangs, the Crips and Bloods, signed a formal truce and pledged to work together to bring peace to the streets.

CHILDREN SAY GOODBYE TO GLENDALE-BURBANK "RED CAR" DURING ITS FINAL WEEK OF OPERATION
JUNE 14, 1955
Some beloved Los Angeles traditions disappeared along with the Red Cars—like field trips to the beach on trolleys filled with singing schoolchildren, or moonlit coastal excursions for adults. Fares averaged less than a penny a mile.

OVERLEAF
INTERSECTION OF OLYMPIC BOULEVARD, FAIRFAX AVENUE AND SAN VICENTE BOULEVARD, LOS ANGELES
SEPTEMBER 1936
A city that grew up in the Auto Age, Los Angeles found itself at a crossroads as the automobile fought for dominance with the once-thriving Red Car system of electric mass transit. When this photo was taken in 1936, the Red Cars were still carrying 59 million people a year—down from a peak in the mid-1920s of 100 million annual passengers. But in a city composed of sprawling suburbs—developments made possible, ironically, by the far-reaching Red Car lines—residents chose the convenience of the private car over mass transit. In 1928 Los Angeles averaged one automobile for every 2.9 persons. By the early 1960s the Red Cars had been retired.

COMINGS AND GOINGS

Movement and momentum have paced Los Angelenos throughout the century as we covered new ground in old ways, and old ground in new ways.

MT. LOWE RAILWAY CAR EN ROUTE TO TOP OF MT. LOWE

CIRCA 1905

Old-timers may remember a popular excursion car that ran to the summit of Mt. Lowe, providing thrilling vistas along a seven-mile route. Started by Professor Thaddeus S. C. Lowe, a Civil War balloonist and inventor, the line was taken over by Henry Huntington and his Pacific Electric Railway Company in 1901. It ascended a straight incline into Rubio Canyon and up to Echo Mountain, and from there wound circuitously to the top of Mt. Lowe, carrying a total of 3.1 million passengers, before it ceased operations in 1937. Portions of the track and structures are still visible to hikers.

"SAVE ANGELS FLIGHT" RIDE AND SIGN, BUNKER HILL

1959

Alternative modes of transportation still exist in Los Angeles, some more dear to the public than others. Known as "the shortest railway in the world," Angels Flight is a funic-

ular originally built at Third Street between Hill and Olive in 1901 to allow the wealthy residents of Bunker Hill and their servants to negotiate the steep incline separating their mansions from the shopping district below. As the area declined, so did use of the railway. In 1969 it was dismantled to make way for the

Bunker Hill urban renewal project. Despite a promise from the City Council to restore the service, the cars sat in storage for a quarter century. Eventually preservationists and the Community Redevelopment Agency won their battle to reopen the beloved funicular a half-block away near Fourth Street, and

Angels Flight was reinstalled and reopened in 1996. For 25 cents a ride, it now carries patrons "into the past" and up the hill from the Grand Central Market to the tony Water-court Plaza.

TEST RUN FOR AERIAL TROLLEY CAR IN BURBANK, CREATED BY JOSEPH WESLEY FAWKES

CIRCA 1912

This idea never found backers—but if it had, the public might be enjoying futuristic monorail travel through the air between Burbank and downtown. In 1910 inventor J. W. Fawkes built a propeller-driven aerial trolley that he claimed would haul passengers at speeds up to 60 miles per hour. To demonstrate, he hung a quarter-mile-long overhead track in his Burbank apricot orchard and invited passengers aboard. Dubbed the Aerial Swallow, the trolley was about 40 feet long and powered by a Franklin air-cooled engine, which turned the propeller. But the prototype topped out at three miles per hour, and investors kept their hands in their pockets.

PACIFIC ELECTRIC RED CARS IN WILMINGTON JUNKYARD, AWAITING SHIPMENT TO JAPAN
1959

In its heyday, the Red Car line was the biggest electric urban rail system in the nation, covering more than a thousand miles from San Fernando to Newport Beach and from Redlands to the ocean. Its demise was in part due to self-interested campaigns waged by automotive and oil companies. But ultimately, consumers chose the privacy and convenience of the automobile. The rail system was profitable in only one of its 60 years of operation and was kept afloat by revenues from the sale of real estate in the areas it served—real estate that was controlled by the railway's land development arm. The railway's business plan was devised in 1901 by its founder, Henry Huntington, then the largest landowner in Southern California. Huntington sold the entire Pacific Electric operation in 1910 to the Southern Pacific Railroad. In this 1959 photo, condemned Red Cars await shipment to Japan, where they were valued for their solid American steel. Many cars were melted down and their steel used in Datsuns and Toyotas that were then exported to the United States. Some of the Red Cars were shipped to Argentina, where they operated for years.

CARPENTER'S SANDWICHES, SUNSET & VINE

1932

Here was a sign of things to come: a 24-hour, drive-up fast-food joint. Restaurateur Harry Carpenter had three drive-ins around Los Angeles in the early 1930s; this one on Sunset and Vine was by far the best known due to its proximity to Hollywood and to the nearby CBS, NBC, Paramount and Goldwyn studios, whose stars were often seen and photographed there. Carpenter's octagonally shaped drive-ins were open around the clock and featured bright lights, large signs and an open front area for quick service.

◀ DRIVE-UP POLIO VACCINATION, LOS ANGELES
CIRCA 1958

By the 1950s the auto obsession had reached full throttle. The polio vaccine, created by Jonas Salk in 1954, was disseminated in Southern California with a particular twist: a drive-up vaccination program. How much easier it was to lure Angelenos to get their shots when they didn't even have to leave their cars!

ROADSIDE TRAFFIC COURT, INGLEWOOD
JULY 1926

A unique car culture was already springing up in Los Angeles in the late 1920s. This curbside scene illustrates frontier justice adapted to the automobile: instant judgment combined with the convenience for all parties of having the matter settled on the spot. The process took 10 minutes total and, as *The Times* noted, "luckless speeders … were kept from cluttering up the regular courts with traffic cases."

110

AUTOS JAM WILSHIRE BOULEVARD
IN BOTH DIRECTIONS

EASTER SUNDAY, 1941

The development of the freeways came none too soon, as evidenced by this traffic jam on Wilshire Boulevard near the Bullocks Wilshire department store, at left. Traffic was a major problem in 1940s Los Angeles, as automobiles had become a way of life, with many families owning two. Motorists who drove in from the suburbs to work or shop created paralyzing traffic jams and horrific parking problems. The parking lot soon became central to city planning, particularly along the shopping mecca of Wilshire Boulevard, which catered to motorists with big parking lots behind each store.

SMOG PROTESTERS AT SEVENTH
AND BROADWAY, LOS ANGELES ▶

1950s

Smog was at its worst in the 1950s when Ivan and Mildred Dugan, early anti-smog warriors shown here in gas masks, took to the streets to protest against noxious air. The backfire from the region's car culture and rapid industrial growth, smog has been a problem in the Los Angeles basin since shortly before World War II. In 1969 a coroner in Los Angeles was able to certify that a murder victim had only recently come to the city because there was no trace of smog in the victim's lungs. Cleaner-burning cars and much tighter local air pollution laws—among the toughest in the country—have now dramatically improved air quality from its low point in the 1950s and '60s.

111

EXAMINING APPLICANTS FOR MOTOR VEHICLE OPERATORS' LICENSES USING SCALE MODELS OF CARS AND ROADS

CIRCA 1930

These labor- and time-intensive exams showed the luxuries of sufficient manpower, relatively few license applicants and uncom-

plicated street grids facing motorists. The Department of Motor Vehicles first issued registrations—191,000 of them statewide—in 1914, when it also began issuing its first permanent license plates. The state now issues 27.5 million registrations per year, 6.1 million of those in Los Angeles County alone.

SWEEPING INTERSECTION OF THE HARBOR (110) AND SANTA MONICA (10) FREEWAYS JUST SOUTHWEST OF DOWNTOWN

NOVEMBER 1980

Essential to the city's sprawling character and its attachment to the automobile was the development of a system of toll-free roadways that would deliver commuters briskly to their destinations—at least in theory. The first freeway, between downtown and Pasadena, opened in 1939. Today the freeways dominate the landscape and the local psyche. The city's largest physical structures, they comprise the one experience most Angelenos have in common. The weekday "rush hours" are anything but, though at other times this transportation system can be impressively swift. The life-lines of the city, L.A.'s 18 freeways—most built before 1970—have spawned a culture of their own, from "SigAlert" traffic jams to drive-by shootings to televised police chases.

◄ **AERIAL VIEW LOOKING EAST OF THE INTERCHANGE OF THE HARBOR (110) AND CENTURY (105) FREEWAYS, SOUTH CENTRAL LOS ANGELES**

1997

Los Angeles' Century Freeway, so named to commemorate 100 years of transportation progress, opened in 1993, the city's newest and, at a cost of $2.2 billion, most expensive highway. Its main purpose was to provide a rapid, congestion-free route to the airport from downtown. The freeway's soaring ramps and lacy architecture—which handily withstood a major earthquake in 1994—can cause even jaded Angelenos to marvel.

COLLAPSE OF INTERSTATE 14 OVERPASS ONTO THE GOLDEN STATE FREEWAY, SEVERAL HOURS AFTER THE EARTHQUAKE

JANUARY 17, 1994

This section of Interstate 14 proved the city's vulnerability when it collapsed during the Northridge earthquake, which staggered the region at 4:31 on a Monday morning. Predawn commuter traffic was uncommonly light, as the disaster occurred on the Martin Luther King holiday. LAPD motorcycle officer Clarence Wayne Dean, who was racing to work to report for emergency duty, was the only fatality in this freeway collapse. In the early morning darkness, Dean did not see that the road had sheared away, and drove off the broken edge. The interchange was renamed in his honor after its reconstruction several months later.

HOWARD HUGHES SITS ATOP HIS PLANE, THE WINGED BULLET, IN WHICH HE SET A WORLD SPEED RECORD, AFTER ITS FORCED LANDING IN A BEET FIELD NEAR SANTA ANA
SEPTEMBER 1935

Hughes had earlier set a world speed record of 352 miles per hour in this plane, but during this flight the fuel mechanism shut down, forcing his emergency landing. Two years later, in a different craft, he set a transcontinental air record of seven hours, 28 minutes. Hughes would go on to become an important force in two of Los Angeles' key industries—aerospace and movies.

UP, UP AND AWAY

Airplanes, pilots and other things that defy gravity.

1910 DOMINGUEZ AIR MEET PARTICIPANTS

JANUARY 1910

America's first international air meet took place just south of Los Angeles, on Dominguez Field near the present-day city of Carson. The highly promoted event drew keen interest, but the nearly 20,000 who attended could not have guessed that the fledging field of aviation would become one of the major industries to shape Los Angeles, along with oil and motion pictures. Within a decade, pioneers like Donald Douglas and the Loughead (later Lockheed) brothers had established the region's first aircraft manufacturing plants. In this view, J. C. Klassen and G. Bentley, mechanic (both standing), along with V. C. Warden, mechanic (kneeling), take a break from the action at the historic event, which took place only seven years after the Wright Brothers' first flight.

DEDICATION OF MINES FIELD, LATER
LOS ANGELES INTERNATIONAL AIRPORT

JUNE 7, 1930

One of the world's largest and busiest airports, Los Angeles International Airport (LAX) each year guides 740,000 landings and takeoffs, handles 64 million passengers and loads and unloads 2 million tons of air cargo, playing a key role in the city's economy. In 1928 the airport was created on 640 acres of bean fields in Westchester. A single 2,000-foot landing strip and two 100-foot hangars were built before this official dedication of the site, then called Mines Field, on June 7, 1930. The control tower in this photo has since been replaced by a $29-million land-mark that rises 289 feet. There have been other expansions, to say the least. In 1946, most airline companies moved their flights and facilities to LAX from a Lockheed-owned facility in the Valley, now called Burbank Air-port, which until then had been the region's busiest. In 1950 the City Council bestowed the name Los Angeles International (LAX).

121

◄ **AMELIA EARHART ATOP HER NEW HIGH-ALTITUDE PLANE, CAPABLE OF FLYING TO 27,500 FEET**

JULY 1936

Earhart, who was a Toluca Lake resident, started her career as a pilot in Los Angeles after taking her first airplane ride with a barnstormer and finding her calling. She paid for flying lessons by driving a gravel truck in Los Angeles and saved for years to buy her own plane. Today Earhart, whose Lockheed 10-E Electra disappeared over the Pacific Ocean in 1937, is warmly remembered as a flier, poet and amateur photographer who typified restless daring and adventuresome spirit.

CHUCK YEAGER WITH BELL X-1 PLANE AT EDWARDS AIR FORCE BASE

APRIL 1950

Edwards Air Force Base, in the Antelope Valley north of Los Angeles, became world famous as a test site for advanced aircraft. Chuck Yeager, the nation's most outstanding experimental test pilot during the 1940s and '50s, gained his greatest fame on October 14, 1947, when he broke the sound barrier while flying an X-1 Bell aircraft over Edwards, known at the time as Muroc Air Force Base. Yeager went on to fly 127 combat missions in Vietnam before retiring in 1975. The plane pictured here, like all of Yeager's craft, was named after his wife.

HOWARD HUGHES' "SPRUCE GOOSE" AS IT WAS FLOATED IN LONG BEACH HARBOR FOR ITS MAIDEN VOYAGE

NOVEMBER 2, 1947

With metal scarce immediately after World War II, aviator and industrialist Howard Hughes turned to lumber to build this experimental craft, originally planned as a giant wooden troop carrier. Despite its name, the plane was made mostly of birch plywood, with little spruce. Its 320-foot wingspan made it the world's largest plane. With Hughes at the controls, the Spruce Goose flew for about a mile over the bay and touched down with a satisfying hiss. It would never fly again. Hughes, a well-known aviator, had started Hughes Aircraft Company in the 1930s as part of a tool company he inherited. He also increased his wealth by purchasing a controlling share in TWA. Hughes Aircraft Co. became a major defense contractor and significant employer in Southern California. The company developed innovations in radar and space communications, missiles and avionics, air defense and industrial electronics before being sold in 1985 to General Motors, which later divested large portions of it. Hughes himself also became an important moviemaker, producing, among other films, *Hell's Angels* (1930), *Front Page* (1931) and *The Outlaw* (1943).

JACK K. NORTHROP AND PILOT EDWARD BELLANDE DISCUSS FLIGHT PLAN OF THE ORIGINAL FLYING WING

1929

A restless innovator named Jack Northrop became another important force in developing the area's aviation industry. Originally partnered with the Lockheed brothers and later with Donald Douglas, Northrop kept launching new companies so he could focus on research and design rather than fulfilling production contracts. Shown here is an early prototype of his unusual Flying Wing, first tested in 1929. It featured all-metal construction and attempted to reduce drag by incorporating the fuselage and tail assembly in the wing itself. Finally perfected in 1943, after Northrop Aircraft had been launched in Hawthorne, it led to many military innovations designed and built by Northrop, including the P-61 (Black Widow) night fighter and the F-16 Reporter, a high-speed photo-reconnaisance monoplane. Here, Northrop is shown at age 34 with pilot Edward Bellande, who went on to work as one of the first fliers for TWA.

◀ **PASSENGER AIRCRAFT BEING ASSEMBLED**
AT DOUGLAS PLANT IN SANTA MONICA
NOVEMBER 1938

Workers assemble the popular DC-3 passenger craft prior to the outbreak of World War II. At around this time, Douglas passenger craft were carrying 95 percent of all U.S. commercial air traffic. But in 1967 Douglas merged with McDonnell aircraft. Thirty years later, the combined company, McDonnell Douglas, was acquired by Boeing Corp., becoming a victim of the post–Cold War consolidation of aerospace companies that ended Southern California's dominance of the aerospace industry and led to the region's steep recession that began in the early 1990s.

WARTIME PRODUCTION PEAKS
AT LOCKHEED FACILITY

1943

Government orders poured in for Lockheed P-38 fighters. The year this photo was taken, nearly 250,000 Angelenos were working in the aircraft industry. The same year, a Department of Labor report noted that "Los Angeles has become the Detroit of the aircraft industry." In fact, Southern California supplied a third of all U.S. aircraft produced during World War II. During this time, P-38s were rolling off the line at more than 13 per day, and total wartime production topped 10,000.

PREPARING TO TRANSPORT THE LOWER SECTION OF THE 100-INCH HOOKER TELESCOPE FROM PASADENA UP TO THE MT. WILSON OBSERVATORY

OCTOBER 1916

The establishment of the world's largest telescope on Mt. Wilson did much to turn the California Institute of Technology (Caltech) in Pasadena into one of the world's preeminent scientific research centers. But getting it to the top of the mountain was no mean feat. Transporting each section first required a truck and then a team of mules, and took two days. The telescope in its entirety weighs 100 tons. A vital eyepiece to the heavens, the telescope was used to make some of the most important discoveries in the history of astronomy, including Edwin Hubble's findings that the universe was continuing to expand and that numerous galaxies outside our own existed. Built by scientist George Ellery Hale with major funding from Los Angeles businessman John D. Hooker, Mt. Wilson's was the largest telescope in the world for 30 years after it opened in November 1917, and it remains in use.

FIRST ROCKET MOTOR TEST, JET PROPULSION LABORATORY, PASADENA

NOVEMBER 15, 1936

Known as the "nativity scene" at JPL, this view captures the rocket motor test that led to the creation of the Jet Propulsion Laboratory. The men pictured—from left to right, Rudolph Schott, A.M.O. Smith, Frank Malina, Ed Forman and John W. Parsons—were Caltech students whose messy rocket experiments had been banished from the campus. In this quiet arroyo, now the site of the world-famous JPL, they succeeded in sustaining a controlled rocket flight for 46 seconds. A respected aeronautics lab grew from there. With the advent of World War II, JPL became involved in military applications of rocket science. Associated with NASA since 1958, it remains a division of Caltech.

THE SPACE SHUTTLE ENTERPRISE MOCK-UP TAKING OFF ATOP 747 FROM EDWARDS AIR FORCE BASE FOR FINAL TEST

OCTOBER 1977

The testing in 1977 of the Enterprise, a space shuttle prototype, was among the most important of the many pioneering activities that took place at Edwards Air Force base, located about 90 miles north of Los Angeles at the western edge of the Mojave Desert. The Enterprise would never fly in space, or even exceed the speed of sound, but it set the stage for sister ships that would. Launched from atop a Boeing 747 at altitudes ranging from 20,000 to 25,000 feet, it made an extraordinarily successful series of five unpowered approach and landing tests, which validated the techniques that would be employed for mankind's first gliding descents from outer space.

SCIENTISTS AT JPL TEST AN AIR BAG DESIGNED TO ASSURE THE SAFE LANDING ON MARS OF THE PATHFINDER SPACECRAFT, WHICH CONTAINS THE SOJOURNER ROVER. THE TESTING AREA, CALLED "THE MARS YARD," SIMULATES THE PLANET'S SURFACE

NOVEMBER 1995

The Jet Propulsion Laboratory in Pasadena has grown into the world's leading planetary exploration laboratory, with an annual budget of more than $1 billion. Space vehicles have been launched to explore Mars, Venus, Jupiter, Saturn, Uranus and Mercury. After the Pathfinder (being tested above) landed safely on Mars on July 4, 1997, Americans spent the summer riveted by the adventures of the spunky Sojourner rover as it explored the Red Planet, beaming down remarkable pictures. However, JPL engineers found the spotlight less enjoyable two years later, when miscalculations led to embarrassing problems with two consecutive Mars probes, the Climate Orbiter and the Polar Lander. The result was a promise from NASA to overhaul its interplanetary exploration programs.

HOLLYWOODLAND SIGN

CIRCA 1923

Built by Harry Chandler in 1923 to promote his new real estate development Hollywood-land, this 50-foot-high wooden sign would become world famous as a symbol of the emerging movie industry. At night the sign was illuminated by 4,000 20-watt bulbs and could be seen from the harbor off San Pedro, 25 miles away. A caretaker lived in a cabin behind the "L." The sign weighed nearly a half-million pounds and cost $21,000 to con-struct—a bit more than $1,600 for each letter. The Hollywood Chamber of Commerce removed the last four letters in 1945.

FUN AND GAMES

The city shows off, to entertain, to amuse, and for the sheer fun and magic of it all.

132

OPENING PREMIERE AT GRAUMAN'S CHINESE THEATRE, 6925 HOLLYWOOD BOULEVARD

1929

Lavish, star-studded movie premieres were practically invented by theater owner Sid Grauman, who used them as publicity magnets for the pictures opening at his Hollywood Boulevard movie palaces. Grauman built the fabulous Chinese Theater in 1927, down the street from his exotic Egyptian Theater (which today houses the American Cinematheque). The first premiere at the Chinese featured the film *Morocco*, starring Marlene Dietrich. The custom of celebrity footprints and handprints in the concrete in front of the theater, now a major tourist attraction, began after Grauman accidentally stepped into wet cement in the courtyard and decided to capitalize on his mistake, Hollywood style. Douglas Fairbanks, Mary Pickford and Norma Talmadge provided the first celebrity footprints.

133

PLATING THE OSCARS

FEBRUARY 1970

These famous statuettes help rivet worldwide attention on Los Angeles each year when the Academy Award ceremonies are held. Though the movie industry in its earliest days was treated with disdain by the L.A. establishment, it quickly became one of the city's most valuable assets. In the 1920s, when audiences were huge and production costs low, it is estimated that a quarter of the population of Hollywood worked directly for the movies. The origin of the Oscar statuette's name remains uncertain. One story has it that when the librarian at the Academy, Margaret Herrick, first saw the statuette, she exclaimed that it looked "just like my uncle Oscar." Purportedly a reporter overheard the remark and ran it in a story, and it stuck. Yet another account claims that Bette Davis nicknamed the figure after her first husband, Harmon Oscar Nelson, Jr.

134

UNITED ARTISTS FOUNDERS DOUGLAS FAIRBANKS, MARY PICKFORD, CHARLIE CHAPLIN AND D. W. GRIFFITH
1919
These three movie stars and filmmaker D. W. Griffith, whose *Birth of a Nation* expanded the perception of what movies could be, created United Artists in order to control distribution of their own independently produced films. Chaplin built his own studios on La Brea Avenue in 1919. Pickford and Fairbanks purchased the Jesse D. Hampton Studio on Santa Monica Boulevard in 1922.

MGM STUDIO ASSISTANT SORTING MAIL FOR MOVIE CELEBRITIES ▶
1939
MGM film stars, including Gable, Crawford, Barrymore, Garbo and others, received tremendous amounts of fan mail, much of which they read and responded to themselves. It was only when volume became extreme that secretaries and others would have to answer on behalf of the stars.

CHILDREN PLAYING AT MAKING MOVIES

1928

Filmmaking took place in plain sight in its earliest years in Los Angeles, on vacant lots rented for the purpose, or on the streets, where daring filmmakers staged outrageous stunts and grabbed footage of the unsuspecting crowds who gathered. That spirit of public playacting is reflected in the heroic saga enacted by these children. The boy in the broad-brimmed hat has apparently vanquished a bad guy, who lies "dead" at his feet, for the adoring little miss on his arm, while the "director" and "cameraman" capture the action. To add another layer to the illusion, these youngsters were probably posed for the picture by photographer Dick Whittington, well known for his Los Angeles "color" shots.

**FILMING ON A DOWNTOWN STREET
FOR THE THRILLER *SHOCK PROOF*
ATTRACTS SIGHTSEERS**

JANUARY 1949

The coming of the studio soundstages meant that much of Hollywood filmmaking disappeared indoors. But sidewalk scenes such as this one, in which Cornel Wilde and Patricia Knight enact a scene shot on location, still remained a part of the city's special character.

Even today, filming on location remains so commonplace in Los Angeles that in some parts of the city, even houses have agents. Despite a recent hemorrhage of film and television activity to money-saving locales in Canada, overall production days in Los Angeles, including commercials, music videos, photo shoots, film and TV, rose nearly 2 percent in 1999 from the previous year.

◄ OZZIE AND HARRIET NELSON WITH SONS DAVID AND RICKY

MAY 1955

Television was still a relatively new medium in 1952, when former bandleader Ozzie Nelson created a show about idealized family life, using his real-life wife and sons on a set that duplicated their Hollywood home. The show ran 14 seasons, becoming the longest-running sitcom ever, and was the first concrete example of the way Hollywood-born popular culture shaped the way Americans throughout the country viewed their own lives. The names "Ozzie and Harriet" are still used to describe the myth of domestic perfection and fully functional family life. Shows like *Father Knows Best* and *Leave It to Beaver* followed in its footsteps. Beginning in 1956, younger son Ricky's real-life career as a rock 'n' roll musician and teen idol gave the show added appeal and further reflected what was going on in the nation.

JOHNNY CARSON AS "CARNAC THE MAGNIFICENT" AND SIDEKICK ED McMAHON

MAY 1992

Johnny Carson helped interpret the emerging city of Los Angeles for the rest of the nation after *The Tonight Show* moved from New York to L.A. in 1972, mirroring an overall trend in the television industry. Carson referred to L.A. constantly in his nightly comedy monologues and made sardonic references to "beautiful downtown Burbank," where the NBC studios were located. In all, Carson's stint on *The Tonight Show* ran for nearly 30 years, from 1962 to 1992, and made him one of the most influential and enduring performers in television. *The Tonight Show* helped launch a thousand stand-up careers, and watching it is still a nightly pre-sleep ritual for viewers nationwide.

**THE BEACH BOYS PERFORM
AT THE HOLLYWOOD BOWL**

NOVEMBER 1963

In the clean-cut pop era of the early '60s, the Beach Boys became a nationwide sensation, helping to ignite the culture of Southern California in the minds of the nation's youth with songs like "Surfin' Safari" and "California Girls." Brothers Dennis, Brian and Carl Wil-

son were teens from Hawthorne, 15 miles southwest of downtown L.A. Brian is credited with masterminding the sophisticated harmonies and arrangements showcased on the group's *Pet Sounds* album, said to have influenced the Beatles, among others.

**FRANK ZAPPA IN HIS STUDIO CITY
HOME STUDIO** ▶

DECEMBER 1989

The diverse, sophisticated music styles of rock iconoclasts like Frank Zappa and his Mothers of Invention, Captain Beefheart, Van Dyke Parks, Canadian-born Joni Mitchell, Arthur Lee and Love and Randy Newman were also a key part of the musical fabric of

Los Angeles. A quirky and brilliant musician and social satirist, Zappa went head-to-head with politicians during Congressional hearings on pornographic lyrics in 1985, later incorporating sound bites from the proceedings into one of his albums. His album *Freak Out* (1966) is considered one of the all-time great rock music albums. Zappa died of prostate cancer in 1993 at the age of 52.

142

THE DOORS: JOHN DENSMORE, ROBBY KRIEGER, JIM MORRISON AND RAY MANZAREK

CIRCA 1969

A quintessential Los Angeles band, the Doors first formed during the summer of 1965 in Venice, coming together under charismatic leader Jim Morrison in a remarkable fusion of creativity and energy. The group took its name from the poet William Blake, who penned the line, "When the doors of perception are cleansed, things will appear to man as they truly are … infinite." The group's hit songs included "Light My Fire," "Love Me Two Times," "L.A. Woman" and "Riders on the Storm." Together with San Francisco groups like the Jefferson Airplane, the Doors helped form an impression among the nation's youthful counterculture that California was the place to be. The band's first significant shows were at the Whisky on the Sunset Strip, shown opposite.

143

CROWDS IN FRONT OF THE WHISKY ON SUNSET BOULEVARD IN WEST HOLLYWOOD

SEPTEMBER 19, 1982

In the 1970s, Los Angeles emerged as the true center of the nation's recording industry. In 1978 alone, the record business pumped an estimated $2 billion into the local economy. Today most of the major labels, such as Warner Bros., Sony and MCA, are linked to movie studios under the umbrella of entertainment conglomerates. Nightclubs like the Whisky on the Sunset Strip are patrolled by talent scouts for the labels, who occasionally sign new acts from among thousands of contenders. In this photo, crowds gather to hear the Plimsouls, a potent Los Angeles power-pop group, on the final night before the Whisky closed down temporarily as a live rock venue in 1982. The club later reopened and continues to be a key venue for showcasing new acts.

144

WALT DISNEY, EDWIN HUBBLE AND SIR JULIAN HUXLEY AT DISNEY STUDIO ON HYPERION AVENUE

DECEMBER 1939

The juxtaposition of cutting-edge arts and sciences in Los Angeles, perhaps exemplified in the twin presences of CalArts and Caltech, is part of the area's unique mix of resources.

In this photo, moviemaker and animator Disney consults with Hubble, one of the world's great astronomers, and Huxley, biologist, author and one of the most noted scientists of the mid-20th century. The men are viewing dinosaur models for the "Rite of Spring" sequence of the movie *Fantasia*, which was finished and released in November 1940.

Because the segment related to the creation of Earth, it is probable that the scientists visited the studio to offer Disney—ever the perfectionist—advice on that sequence.

**MATT GROENING AT WORK ON
HIS CARTOON STRIP "LIFE IN HELL,"
IN HIS VENICE HOME STUDIO**

CIRCA 1986

L.A.'s cross-pollinating media have incubated the success of creatives-turned-conglomerates like cartoonist Matt Groening (which, he likes to note, rhymes with "complaining").

Groening started out in 1980 sketching the irreverent weekly comic strip "Life in Hell," about a trio of alienated rabbits and the identical twins/lovers Akbar and Jeff, which still appears in the alternative paper *L.A. Weekly* and 250 others. In 1987 he debuted *The Simpsons* as a series of animated shorts on *The Tracey Ullman Show*. The dysfunctional cartoon family got its own show in 1989 and has become television's longest-running animated series, paving the way for other animators to create smart, sardonic and topical fare. "Most grown-ups forget what it was like to be a kid," said Groening in a recent interview. "I vowed I would never forget."

◄ **SIGN PAINTERS FINISH A MURAL OF CLINT EASTWOOD ON SUNSET BOULEVARD**
FEBRUARY 1996

In the 1970s and '80s, Clint Eastwood became associated with one of Hollywood's most controversial exports—violent entertainment. In action pictures like *Dirty Harry* and Westerns like *The Outlaw Josie Wales*—a representation of which appears here—Eastwood portrayed rebellious loners bent on meting out justice with a gun. But Eastwood also became celebrated as the director of movies with considerable artistic merit, including *Bird*, his paean to jazz great Charlie Parker, and *Unforgiven*, an anti-violence Western that won the 1992 Oscar for best picture. A California native, Eastwood dug swimming pools for a living before signing on as a contract player at Universal in the 1950s. Like Ronald Reagan and Sonny Bono, he entered politics, but only briefly—in a two-year term as mayor of Carmel, his adopted hometown. The election, in 1986, drew twice the usual voter turnout, and Eastwood won by a landslide 72 percent.

UNOCAL ENTRY IN ROSE PARADE
JANUARY 2000

Via its annual Rose Parade, Los Angeles continues to flaunt its fabled climate before a television audience estimated at 365 million viewers in 2000—most of whom must actually suffer through a real winter. The floats are now corporate-branded extravaganzas that feature hydraulics and microchips. But as ever, they are entirely decorated with fresh flowers and other organic material. About 750,000 people attend each year, with many camping along the parade route in Pasadena overnight. At the 111th annual Tournament of Roses Parade on New Year's Day 2000, it rained for the first time since 1955.

A GUARD TAKES A BREAK AT THE METRO RAIL STATION, HOLLYWOOD AND VINE
JUNE 1999

The specter of the automobile haunts this mass transit worker, even at the subway station. A 1996 survey, taken three years before the MTA extended its Red Line through Hollywood and opened new stations like this one, reported that only 5 percent of Southern California commuters used mass transit.

PRESENT TENSE

At the beginning of a new century, we assess the past and imagine the future.

THE GETTY CENTER ON A CLEAR, WINDY DAY, WITH SNOWCAPPED MT. SAN JACINTO VISIBLE ON THE HORIZON

1998

The opening of the new $1-billion Getty Center museum was heralded as a true cultural coming of age for Los Angeles, as it drew unprecedented worldwide attention in art and architecture circles. Offering free admission to its arts and antiquities galleries, as well as lavish gardens and panoramic city views, the museum was so popular with

tourists and locals alike during its first year that it was compelled to buy ads discouraging attendance. The six-building complex, designed by Richard Meier in muted Modernist style with travertine and undulating glass, was built from the fortune of oil baron J. Paul Getty. Architect Meier said he hoped the arts monument would bring a sense of "rootedness" to a city that once exemplified the new and transitory.

STAPLES CENTER AT 11TH AND FIGUEROA STREETS, DOWNTOWN

1999

Touted as a showpiece facility central to revitalizing the long-neglected downtown area, this sleekly designed $375-million sports and entertainment complex opened in late 1999, becoming the new home to L.A.'s Lakers and Clippers basketball teams and Kings hockey team. The arena features an eight-sided scoreboard and display video, 20,000 seats, 55 public restrooms and 24 refreshment stands and is expected to stimulate business downtown. With its entire mid-level reserved for private dining clubs and luxury suites costing as much as $300,000 a year, the complex has sparked much public debate about its perceived elitism. Big-name concerts, including shows by Bruce Springsteen and the Eagles, and the Democratic Convention, booked for August 2000, have helped raise the center's profile.

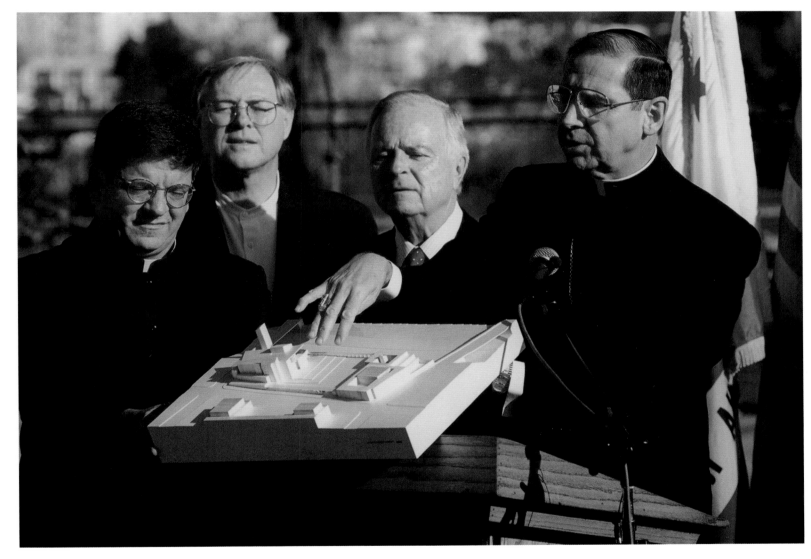

CARDINAL MAHONY DISPLAYS A MODEL OF THE NEW CATHEDRAL OF OUR LADY OF THE ANGELS

DECEMBER 1996

Another point of pride in the downtown revitalization effort is the new $163-million Roman Catholic cathedral, rising from a hill-top downtown at the corner of Grand and Temple streets, which will serve the archdiocese of Los Angeles—the nation's most populous. The new Cathedral of Our Lady of the Angels is expected to be completed by 2002. Located a half mile from historic St. Vibiana's, which suffered earthquake damage in 1994, the new 3,000-seat cathedral features a 120-foot bell tower. Mayor Richard Riordan, second from right, with Monsignor Terrance Fleming, County Supervisor Mike Antonovich and Cardinal Roger M. Mahony, has called it "a giant step forward in the renaissance of downtown Los Angeles." Some Catholics have complained that the money could have been better spent serving the poor. Nearby on Grand Street, ground was broken in December 1999 for the Frank Gehry–designed Walt Disney Concert Hall, and together the two new structures are expected to help advance a cultural transformation of the city's downtown.

158

DANCER PERFORMS AT THAI TOWN OPENING CEREMONIES

JANUARY 2000

Newcomers, who transformed the landscape of Los Angeles throughout the 20th century with their rich cultural influences, are expected to lead a major population increase projected for the first 20 years of the 21st century. Thai immigrants first began arriving in large numbers in Los Angeles in the 1960s, and Southern California today has more than 80,000 Thai residents—the largest concentration outside Thailand. The Los Angeles City Council recently designated a six-block area of east Hollywood as Thai Town, creating the first official Thai Town in the nation. Community organizers hope it will bring cultural awareness and economic benefits. However, the actual population of the area, on Hollywood Boulevard between Western and Normandie, is a mix of Thai, Armenian, Russian, Guatemalan and Mexican residents and business owners—a good example of the increasingly multicultural character of the city.

159

BELMONT LEARNING COMPLEX, UNDER CONSTRUCTION AT BEAUDRY AVENUE AND FIRST STREET DOWNTOWN

DECEMBER 1999

Meeting the basic educational needs of a growing population continues to present a serious challenge to Los Angeles leaders. The Belmont Learning Complex could have accommodated 5,000 students, but the Los Angeles school board abandoned the project shortly after this photo was taken, after environmental hazards made it unfeasible. Meanwhile, the existing Belmont High School overflows with more than 4,500 students, while thousands more from the downtown area are bused to the San Fernando Valley every day for school. More than $200 million had been sunk into the Belmont project, making it the most expensive high school in the nation's history, before construction was halted due to potentially explosive gases leaking from the former oil field on which it was situated. Now school officials face finding another solution for students in the predominantly Latino neighborhood.

160

**NIGHT FALLS ON EXPERIMENTAL
DOME VILLAGE FOR THE HOMELESS**

DECEMBER 1994

Located near the Eighth Street offramp of the Harbor Freeway, these fiberglass domes offer low-cost urban shelter to the homeless—a dramatic contrast to the financial towers of power on Bunker Hill. Opened in late 1993 as a yearlong experiment in communal living after ARCO provided a $250,000 grant, the village has survived more than six years. After a rocky start and much turnover, the residents have achieved some stability and serenity. The once-bleak site now features lawns, flower beds and fruit trees. Volunteers, including USC students and senior citizens, help residents tend gardens.

**SPELLING MANSION IN HOLMBY HILLS
DURING CONSTRUCTION**

1988

A tale of two cities is told by Los Angeles' craze for lavish new luxury housing. Shown here is arguably the city's most extreme example, a 56,000-square-foot mansion for two: television producer Aaron Spelling and his wife, Candy. Under construction for more than five years, the house features a bowling alley and a doll museum. Sales of Los Angeles–area homes costing $1 million or more reached record levels in 1999, up 34 percent from the previous peak in 1998.

◀ **SUBWAY PASSENGERS EXIT THE RED LINE AT THE NEW WESTERN AND WILSHIRE STATION ON ITS OPENING DAY**

JULY 1996

The subway is either a step forward in Los Angeles' evolution as a great city, or an appalling financial boondoggle, depending on whom you ask. Voters fed up by corruption and cost overruns pulled the plug in 1998, decreeing that the Red Line would end with stations that open in Hollywood, Universal City and North Hollywood in June 2000. The new stations are expected to stimulate business in surrounding areas, but will not likely do much to alleviate freeway congestion in a sprawling city where residents remain addicted to their private cars.

CLASSIC CARS RECEIVE THEIR DUE AT THE ANNUAL BLESSING OF THE CARS, HELD IN GLENDALE'S VERDUGO PARK

JUNE 1996

Despite MTA warnings that average freeway speeds may slow to 10 mph by 2015, Angelenos are unlikely to give up their cars. The city's zeal for wheels is exemplified at this annual rockabilly music fest and classic car show, where priests sprinkle holy water into the radiators of restored 1950s relics and offer prayers that they will remain roadworthy. Shown here is Father Charles Leuras of Silver Lake, who sports hot rod–inspired flames at the bottom of his stole.

LOS ANGELES GLITTERS BELOW AS CAR HEADLIGHTS ARC ALONG MULHOLLAND DRIVE

Less than a century has passed since Mulholland built his aqueduct, and within that time, Los Angeles has come to symbolize countless urgent dreams that came true—a place that succeeded beyond the wildest of them. Los Angeles has become a true millennial city—an incubator for cutting-edge trends and developments, a place of dizzying promise and daunting extremes. Its population, ever growing, has proven uniquely adept at surmounting obstacles and adapting to change—crucial qualities in facing the chal-

lenges to come. But while our heads tell us to look constantly toward the future, in our hearts we yearn for a connection with the past. The photographs in this book have told the story of a city in constant flux, a city that changes so quickly that we can scarcely find landmarks or recognize neighborhoods from one decade to the next, as new cultures and new currents transform them. These photographs, then, are all the more precious— fascinating glimpses of an evanescent history. It's a story that comes clearer the closer you get to it, and one that we ourselves are part of, for as long as we live here.

LOS ANGELES: AN ABRIDGED TIMELINE

OLYMPICS ENTHUSIASTS PROMOTE THE CITY'S FIRST GAMES

PRE-1900

1781: 44 settlers from Mexico arrive to open a trading outpost for Spain and call it El Pueblo de la Reina de Los Angeles.

1826: First band of Americans comes overland to the pueblo.

1876: The Southern Pacific Railway reaches Los Angeles.

1881: Downtown Los Angeles gets its first electric lights.

1877: Telephone service introduced to Los Angeles.

1886: A railroad price war sends fares to Los Angeles as low as $8, enticing thousands of settlers.

1890: First Rose Parade held in Pasadena.

1900

POPULATIONS:
LOS ANGELES CITY: 102,479
LOS ANGELES COUNTY: 170,298

1901: Henry Huntington establishes the Pacific Electric Railway Co. to provide regional transportation and, more importantly, sell real estate.

1907: The first movie is made in the region with the filming of the second half of *The Count of Monte Cristo*.

1910

CITY: 310,198
COUNTY: 504,131

1910: The first international air meet in the United States draws nearly 20,000 onlookers to Dominguez Field, near the present-day city of Carson.

1913: The Los Angeles Aqueduct is completed; opening day ceremonies attract an estimated 40,000 residents.

1914: The new Los Angeles port opens in San Pedro, five years after city annexes the territory and just in time to capitalize on burgeoning traffic through the newly completed Panama Canal.

1915: San Fernando Valley residents vote to annex to Los Angeles by a margin of 681 to 25.

1920

CITY: 576,673
COUNTY: 936,455

1924: City voters approve plans for highways into the suburbs as Los Angeles moves ahead of San Francisco to become the most populous city in California.

1928: The newly built City Hall at First and Spring streets opens.

1929: The film industry holds its first-ever Academy Awards, later to be known simply as "the Oscars," at the Hotel Roosevelt on Hollywood Boulevard.

1930

CITY: 1,238,048
COUNTY: 2,208,492

1930: Mines Field, which grew to become Los Angeles International Airport, opens on 640 acres of bean fields in Westchester.

1932: City hosts the 10th Modern Olympics at the Coliseum in Exposition Park.

1939: Union Station opens.
On New Year's Eve, initial six-mile stretch of the Arroyo Seco Parkway (now the Pasadena Freeway) opens just hours before the rush to the Rose Parade, becoming the first freeway in the West.

1940

CITY: 1,504,277
COUNTY: 2,785,643

1941: World War II brings a boom to the aircraft industry with an immediate infusion of $550 million worth of orders to local manufacturers.

1942: Expulsion of 110,000 Japanese Americans to internment camps begins.

1943: Five nights of attacks by American servicemen on local Latino men, the so-called "Zoot Suit Riots," rock the city.

1944: The first Japanese internees are released from camps.

1946: Parking meters are introduced in the city.
The Cleveland Rams move to Los Angeles.

1948: Smog fighting efforts begin.

1949: The nation's first four-level freeway interchange opens, connecting the Hollywood, Pasadena, Harbor and Santa Ana freeways.

COWBOY ACTOR WILLIAM S. HART ON LOCATION AT INCEVILLE IN SANTA MONICA, CIRCA 1920

LOS ANGELES AQUEDUCT ON OPENING DAY, NOVEMBER 5, 1913

CREATING LOCAL TELEVISION, CIRCA 1941

THE GETTY MUSEUM IN BRENTWOOD

1950

CITY: 1,970,358
COUNTY: 4,151,687

1952: NBC opens its Burbank television studio.

1955: Disneyland opens, increasing the region's lure as an international tourist mecca.

1958: The Brooklyn Dodgers move to Los Angeles.

1959: Citizen groups save the Watts Towers from demolition.

1960

CITY: 2,461,595
COUNTY: 6,038,771

1961: The last surviving piece of the Pacific Electric Railway's "Red Car" transit system shuts down.

1964: The Dorothy Chandler Pavilion opens at the Music Center.

1965: The Los Angeles County Museum of Art opens on Wilshire Boulevard.

The Watts Riots erupt, causing the deaths of 34 and damages of $40 million.

1970

CITY: 2,811,801
COUNTY: 7,055,800

1973: Tom Bradley defeats Sam Yorty to become Los Angeles' first black mayor.

1975: The Bloods, a Los Angeles street gang, form.

1980

CITY: 2,967,000
COUNTY: 7,477,503

1984: The city is host to the Summer Olympics. Despite initial concern among residents, the painstaking preparations stave off a much-feared traffic nightmare.

1990

CITY: 3,485,390
COUNTY: 8,769,944

1990: End of the Cold War spells end of huge defense contracts at area aerospace companies, leading to massive layoffs, plant closings and a wave of mergers that virtually decimate what had been the region's principal industry for decades.

1992: Urban rioting, the worst in the nation's history, consumes the city for five days, leaving 51 dead and 2,116 wounded.

1993: The $2.2-billion Century Freeway improves access to Los Angeles International Airport.

The Red Line subway system opens.

1994: The 6.0-magnitude Northridge earthquake stuns a sleeping city on Jan. 17, killing 57. With damages of $27 billion, it ranks as the nation's most costly natural disaster.

1995: The Los Angeles Rams football team moves to St. Louis and goes on to win the Super Bowl five years later.

1997: The $1-billion Getty Center opens as the most expensive art institution ever built in the United States.

2000

Los Angeles city population expected to hit more than 3.6 million; Los Angeles County population estimated to reach 10 million.

AREA NEAR MIRACLE MILE DISTRICT BURNS DURING THE RIOTS OF APRIL 1992

ACKNOWLEDGMENTS

168

THE PHOTOGRAPHS IN THIS BOOK WERE SELECTED from a wide range of photo archives throughout the Los Angeles area. Some of these images have never been published. Others, particularly news photos from the *Los Angeles Times* archive, are shown in their original full frame, revealing, in many cases, details and nuances that were not shown when the pictures were originally published in the newspaper.

Our heartfelt appreciation is due dozens of people who lent substantial intellectual, professional and emotional support to this project. Members of the editorial library staff at the *Los Angeles Times*, including Gay Raszkiewicz, Mildred Simpson, Dorothy Ingebretsen, Suzanne Oatey and Laura Ugalde, provided invaluable help in our research. *Los Angeles Times* photographers Bob Carey, Bob Chamberlin, Carolyn Cole, Ken Lubas, Kirk McKoy, Rick Meyer, Perry C. Riddle, Al Seib and Ted S. Warren generously provided copies of their work for inclusion here, and Larry Armstrong, Matt Randall and Kathy Kottwitz graciously aided that process.

Dan Lewis, curator of American historical manuscripts at the Huntington Library, shepherded the project during its initial stages, and we thank him for providing much of the book's preliminary research and development. During his involvement on the project, Dan was advised by Huntington Library colleagues Martin Ridge, Jennifer Watts, Kate McGinn and Erin Wardlow, and he remains grateful for their support. Thanks also to John LaMartine.

Others who deserve our thanks include: Gloria Ricci Lothrop, W. P. Whitsett professor of California history at California State University, Northridge; Dace Taube, curator, Regional History Center, Department of Special Collections, USC; Carolyn Kozo Cole, senior librarian, Photograph Collection, Los Angeles Public Library; Leonard and Dale Pitt, authors of *Los Angeles A to Z*; John Cahoon, Seaver Center for Western History Research; Tom Sitton, Natural History Museum of Los Angeles County; Julio Gonzalez, archivist, The Music Center Operating Company; Morgan Yates, archivist, Automobile Club of Southern California; Debbie Henderson and Cameron Trowbridge, archivists, Japanese American National Museum; Ellen Dibble and Mary Jane Strickland, Burbank Historical Society; Rhoda Monkarsh, executive director, Jewish Home for the Aging; Mark Reed, micrographics coordinator, Community Redevelopment Agency; Nik Wheeler, photographer; Geary Chansley, Chansley Entertainment Archives; Henry Diltz, photographer; Jay Jones, acting archivist, Los Angeles City Archives; Bill Estrada, Olvera Street State Historic Park; David Smith, Walt Disney Archives; Paul Soifer, consulting historian, Los Angeles Department of Water and Power; Ray Costa, Costa Communications/*Low Rider* magazine; Manny Medina-Kauwe, graphics supervisor, The Port of Los Angeles; and Carolyn and Peter Strickler.

We were also aided by numerous staff members at other institutions, including Academy of Motion Picture Arts & Sciences, Beverly Hills Public Library, Burbank Public Library, California African-American Museum, Glendale Public Library, Jet Propulsion Laboratory, Pasadena Historical Museum, Pasadena Public Library, Southern California Library for Social Studies and Research, and St. Vincent Medical Center Historical Conservancy.

We have tried as thoroughly as possible to determine the date, origin and historical significance of each of the photographs reproduced here. As with any project of this type, any errors, omissions, misinterpretations or misplaced attributions are ours. And while we hope there are none, we apologize in advance in the event that some are uncovered and promise corrections in subsequent printings.

PHOTOGRAPHY

All images in this book are from the *Los Angeles Times* Editorial Library except for images on the following pages, which are courtesy of:

171

172

HOLLENBECK PARK

CIRCA 1910

This tranquil oasis was one of the city's first parks, established through the efforts of William Workman, mayor of Los Angeles from 1886–88, and local resident Mrs. J. E. Hollenbeck, who donated two-thirds of the land. A tireless city booster during the 1880s and 1890s, Workman laid the groundwork for the creation of the park over a two-year span beginning in 1889. It still exists, at 415 S. St. Louis Street in Boyle Heights, but in a radically changed neighborhood with cars now zooming past on the adjacent Golden State Freeway.

The text of this book is set in Californian, a typeface designed originally by Frederic W. Goudy in 1938 for private use by the University of California Press. The sans-serif typeface is Nobel, an "enlivened" version of Futura created in 1929 by Sjoerd Henrik de Roos and revived by Tobias Frere-Jones in 1993. Both typefaces were produced in digital form by the Font Bureau, in Boston, Massachusetts. The type was set by Michael Diehl.

OTHER BOOKS FROM THE LOS ANGELES TIMES

DRAWING THE LINE

by Paul Conrad

Two hundred drawings, spanning the period from the late 1960s to President Clinton's impeachment trial, from America's premier political cartoonist. $25.45

ETERNALLY YOURS

by Jack Smith

Who can forget Jack Smith, the *Los Angeles Times'* columnist for nearly 40 years? When he died in 1996, we all lost a treasure. But at least his words survived. In this volume, Jack's widow, Denise, and his sons, Curt and Doug, have collected some of their favorite columns, including those that explain Jack's life as well as his death. $16.95

CURBSIDE L.A.

AN OFFBEAT GUIDE TO THE CITY OF ANGELS

by Cecilia Rasmussen

Enjoy a truly eclectic tour of Los Angeles. Explore the L.A. you've not seen with enticing excursions into the city's peerless history and diversity. $19.45

DAY HIKERS' GUIDE TO SOUTHERN CALIFORNIA

by John McKinney

Walks in Southern California, from the simply scenic to the challenging, as described by *Los Angeles Times* hiking columnist and author John McKinney. $16.45

52 WEEKS IN THE CALIFORNIA GARDEN

by Robert Smaus

How to make the most of your garden by the foremost authority on gardening in Southern California. $17.45

GOD AND MR. GOMEZ

by Jack Smith

The hilarious account of how Jack and Denise Smith learned that it would take both God and Mr. Gomez to build their vacation dream home in Baja California. $16.95

HIGH EXPOSURE / HOLLYWOOD LIVES

FOUND PHOTOS FROM THE ARCHIVES OF THE *LOS ANGELES TIMES*

by Amanda Parsons

In this beautiful hardcover book you'll see photographs of Marilyn Monroe, Liz Taylor, Mae West, Jane Russell, Frank Sinatra, Rita Hayworth, Errol Flynn and scores more stars at the height, and sometimes the depth, of their Hollywood lives. $29.95

L.A. UNCONVENTIONAL

by Cecilia Rasmussen

Where some people see roadblocks, others, such as the men and women in this volume, see possibility, opportunity and excitement. $30.95

LAST OF THE BEST

90 COLUMNS FROM THE 1990s BY THE LATE JIM MURRAY

The best of Jim's columns from the last decade of his life are included in this paperback volume compiled by *Times* Sports Editor Bill Dwyre and featuring a foreword by Dodger legend Tommy Lasorda. $19.45

THE GREAT ONES

by Jim Murray

The top men and women of the sports world written about as only this late, great sports columnist could. Foreword by Arnold Palmer. $24.45

LOW-FAT KITCHEN

by Donna Deane

From the pages of the *Los Angeles Times* Food Section come more than 110 recipes that use fresh food flavor, not fat, to satisfy your taste buds. $20.45

SOS RECIPES

30 YEARS OF REQUESTS

by Rose Dosti

This best-selling hard-cover book offers hundreds of tried-and-true recipes for all-time favorite dishes that literally range from soup to nuts. $19.45

TO ORDER, CALL (800) 246-4042 OR VISIT OUR WEB SITE AT HTTP://WWW.LATIMES.COM/BOOKSTORE